Test Yourself

Social Psychology

D0574043

Test Yourself... Psychology Series

Test Yourself

Social Psychology

Dominic Upton and Penney Upton

Multiple-Choice Questions prepared by Laura Scurlock-Evans

LearningMatters

First published in 2011 by Learning Matters Ltd

All rights reserved. No part of this publication may be reproduced, stored in a retrieval system, or transmitted in any form or by any means, electronic, mechanical, photocopying, recording, or otherwise, without prior permission in writing from Learning Matters.

© 2011 Dominic Upton and Penney Upton; MCQs © Learning Matters Ltd

British Library Cataloguing in Publication Data
A CIP record for this book is available from the British Library

ISBN: 978 0 85725 653 9

This book is also available in the following e-book formats:
Adobe ebook ISBN: 978 0 85725 655 3
ePUB book ISBN: 978 0 85725 654 6
Kindle ISBN: 978 0 85725 656 0

The right of Dominic Upton and Penney Upton to be identified as Authors of this Work has been asserted by them in accordance with the Copyright, Designs and Patents Act 1988.

Cover design by Toucan Design
Text design by Toucan Design
Project Management by Deer Park Productions, Tavistock, Devon
Typeset by Pantek Media, Maidstone, Kent
Printed and bound in Great Britain by Bell & Bain Ltd, Glasgow

Learning Matters Ltd
20 Cathedral Yard
Exeter
EX1 1HB
Tel: 01392 215560
info@learningmatters.co.uk
www.learningmatters.co.uk

Contents

Acknowledgements

The production of this series has been a rapid process with an apparent deadline at almost every turn. We are therefore grateful to colleagues both from Learning Matters (Julia Morris and Helen Fairlie) and the University of Worcester for making this process so smooth and (relatively) effortless. In particular we wish to thank our colleagues for providing many of the questions, specifically:

- Biological Psychology: Emma Preece
- Cognitive Psychology: Emma Preece
- Developmental Psychology: Charlotte Taylor
- Personality and Individual Differences: Daniel Kay
- Research Methods and Design in Psychology: Laura Scurlock-Evans
- Social Psychology: Laura Scurlock-Evans

Finally, we must, once again, thank our children (Gabriel, Rosie and Francesca) for not being as demanding as usual during the process of writing and development.

Introduction

Psychology is one of the most exciting subjects that you can study at university in the twenty-first century. A degree in psychology helps you to understand and explain thought, emotion and behaviour. You can then apply this knowledge to a range of issues in everyday life including health and well-being, performance in the workplace, education – in fact any aspect of life you can think of! However, a degree in psychology gives you much more than a set of 'facts' about mind and behaviour; it will also equip you with a wide range of skills and knowledge. Some of these, such as critical thinking and essay writing, have much in common with humanities subjects, while others such as hypothesis testing and numeracy are scientific in nature. This broad-based skill set prepares you exceptionally well for the workplace – whether or not your chosen profession is in psychology. Indeed, recent evidence suggests employers appreciate the skills and knowledge of psychology graduates. A psychology degree really can help you get ahead of the crowd. However, in order to reach this position of excellence, you need to develop your skills and knowledge fully and ensure you complete your degree to your highest ability.

This book is designed to enable you, as a psychology student, to maximise your learning potential by assessing your level of understanding and your confidence and competence in social psychology, one of the core knowledge domains for psychology. It does this by providing you with essential practice in the types of questions you will encounter in your formal university assessments. It will also help you make sense of your results and identify your strengths and weaknesses. This book is one part of a series of books designed to assist you with learning and developing your knowledge of psychology. The series includes books on:

- Biological Psychology
- Cognitive Psychology
- Developmental Psychology
- Personality and Individual Differences
- Research Methods and Design in Psychology
- Social Psychology

In order to support your learning this book includes over 200 targeted Multiple-Choice Questions (MCQs) and Extended Multiple-Choice Questions (EMCQs) that have been carefully put together to help assess your depth of knowledge of social psychology. The MCQs are split into two formats: the foundation level questions are about your level of understanding of the key principles and components of key areas in psychology.

Hopefully, within these questions you should recognise the correct answer from the four options. The advanced level questions require more than simple recognition – some will require recall of key information, some will require application of this information and others will require synthesis of information. At the end of each chapter you will find a set of essay question covering each of the topics. These are typical of the kinds of question that you are likely to encounter during your studies. In each chapter, the first essay question is broken down for you using a concept map, which is intended to help you develop a detailed answer to the question. Each of the concept maps is shaded to show you how topics link together, and includes cross-references to relevant MCQs in the chapter. You should be able to see a progression in your learning from the foundation to the advanced MCQs, to the extended MCQs and finally the essay questions. The book is divided up into 11 chapters and your social psychology module is likely to have been divided into similar topic areas. However, do not let this restrict your thinking in relation to social psychology: these topics interact. The sample essay questions, which complement the questions provided in the chapter, will help you to make the links between different topic areas. You will find the answers to all of the MCQs and EMCQs at the end of the book. There is a separate table of answers for each chapter; use the self monitoring column in each of the tables to write down your own results, coding correct answers as NC, incorrect answers as NI and any you did not respond to as NR. You can then use the table on page 107 to analyse your results.

The aim of the book is not only to help you revise for your exams, it is also intended to help with your learning. However, it is not intended to replace lectures, seminars and tutorials, or to supersede the book chapters and journal articles signposted by your lecturers. What this book can do, however, is set you off on a sound footing for your revision and preparation for your exams. In order to help you to consolidate your learning, the book also contains tips on how to approach MCQ assessments and how you can use the material in this text to assess, *and enhance,* your knowledge base and level of understanding.

Now you know the reasons behind this book and how it will enhance your success, it is time for you to move on to the questions – let the fun begin!

Assessing your interest, competence and confidence

The aim of this book is to help you to maximise your learning potential by assessing your level of understanding, confidence and competence in core issues in psychology. So how does it do this?

Assessing someone's knowledge of a subject through MCQs might at first glance seem fairly straightforward: typically the MCQ consists of a question, one correct answer and one or more incorrect answers, sometimes called distractors. For example, in this book each question has one right answer and three distractors. The goal of an MCQ test is for you to get every question right and so show just how much knowledge you have. However, because you are given a number of answers to select from, you might be able to choose the right answer either by guessing or by simple a process of elimination – in other words by knowing what is not the right answer. For this reason it is sometimes argued that MCQs only test knowledge of facts rather than in-depth understanding of a subject. However, there is increasing evidence that MCQs can also be valuable at a much higher level of learning, if used in the right way (see, for example, Gardner-Medwin and Gahan, 2003). They can help you to develop as a self-reflective learner who is able to recognise the interest you have in a subject matter as well as your level of competence and confidence in your own knowledge.

MCQs can help you gauge your interest, competence and confidence in the following way. It has been suggested (Howell, 1982) that there are four possible states of knowledge (see Table 1). Firstly, it is possible that you do not know something and are not aware of this lack of knowledge. This describes the naive learner – think back to your first week at university when you were a 'fresher' student and had not yet begun your psychology course. Even if you had done psychology at A level, you were probably feeling a little self-conscious and uncertain in this new learning environment. During the first encounter in a new learning situation most of us feel tentative and unsure of ourselves; this is because we don't yet know what it is we don't know – although to feel this lack of certainty suggests that we know there is something we don't know, even if we don't yet know what this is! In contrast, some people appear to be confident and at ease even in new learning situations; this is not usually because they already know everything but rather because they too do not yet know what it is they do not know – but they have yet to even acknowledge that there is a gap in their knowledge. The next step on from this 'unconscious non-competence' is 'conscious non-competence'; once you started your psychology course you began to realise what the gaps were in your knowledge – you now knew what you didn't know! While this can be an uncomfortable feeling, it is important for the learning process that this acknowledgement of a gap in knowledge is made, because it is the first step in reaching the next level of learning – that of a 'conscious competent' learner. In other words you need to know what the gap in your knowledge is so that you can fill it.

Table 1 Consciousness and competence in learning

	Unconscious	**Conscious**
Non-competent	You don't know something and are not aware that you lack this knowledge/skill.	You don't know something and are aware that you lack this knowledge/skill.
Competent	You know something but are not aware of your knowledge/skill.	You know something and are aware of your knowledge/skill.

One of the ways this book can help you move from unconscious non-competency to conscious competency should by now be clear – it can help you identify the gaps in your knowledge. However, if used properly it can do much more; it can also help you to assess your consciousness and competence in this knowledge.

When you answer an MCQ, you will no doubt have a feeling about how confident you are about your answer: 'I know the answer to question 1 is A. Question 2 I am not so sure about. I am certain the answer is not C or D, so it must be A or B. Question 3, I haven't got a clue so I will say D – but that is a complete guess.' Sound familiar? Some questions you know the answers to, you have that knowledge and know you have it; other questions you are less confident about but think you may know which (if not all) are the distractors, while for others you know this is something you just don't know. Making use of this feeling of confidence will help you become a more reflective – and therefore effective – learner.

Perhaps by now you are wondering where we are going with this and how any of this can help you learn. 'Surely all that matters is whether or not I get the answers right? Does that show I have knowledge?' Indeed it may well do and certainly, if you are confident in your answers, then yes it does. But what if you were not sure? What if your guess of D for our fictional question 3 above was correct? What if you were able to complete all the MCQs in a test and score enough to pass – but every single answer was a guess? Do you really know and understand psychology because you have performed well – and will you be able to do the same again if you retake the test next week? Take a look back at Table 1. If you are relying on guesswork and hit upon the answer by accident you might perform well without actually understanding how you know the answer, or that you even knew it (unconscious competence), or you may not realise you don't know something (unconscious non-competence). According to this approach to using MCQs what is important is not how many answers you get right, but whether or not you acknowledge your confidence in the answer you give: it is better to get a wrong answer and acknowledge it is wrong (so as to work on filling that gap).

Therefore what we recommend you do when completing the MCQs is this: for each answer you give, think about how confident you are that it is right. You might want to rate each of your answers on the following scale:

3:   I am confident this is the right answer.

2:   I am not sure, but I think this is the right answer.

1:   I am not sure, but I think this is the wrong answer.

0:   I am confident this is the wrong answer.

Using this system of rating your confidence will help you learn for yourself both what you know and what you don't know. You will become a conscious learner through the self-directed activities contained in this book. Reflection reinforces the links between different areas of your learning and knowledge and strengthens your ability to *justify* an answer, so enabling you to perform to the best of your ability.

References

Gardner-Medwin, A.R. and Gahan, M. (2003) *Formative and Summative Confidence-Based Assessment*, Proceedings of 7th International Computer-Aided Assessment Conference, Loughborough, UK, July, pp. 147–55.

Howell, W. C. (1982) 'An overview of models, methods, and problems', in W.C. Howell and E.A. Fleishman (eds), *Human performance and productivity, Vol. 2: Information processing and decision making.* Hillsdale, NJ: Erlbaum.

Tips for success: how to succeed in your assessments

This book, part of a comprehensive new series, will help you achieve your psychology aspirations. It is designed to assess your knowledge so that you can review your current level of performance and where you need to spend more time and effort reviewing and revising material. However, it hopes to do more than this – it aims to assist you with your learning so it not only acts as an assessor of performance but as an aid to learning. Obviously, it is not a replacement for every single text, journal article, presentation and abstract you will read and review during the course of your degree programme. Similarly, it is in no way a replacement for your lectures, seminars or additional reading – it should complement all of this material. However, it will also add something to all of this other material: learning is assisted by reviewing and assessing and this is what this text aims to do – help you learn through assessing your learning.

The focus throughout this book, as it is in all of the books in this series, is on how you should approach and consider your topics in relation to assessment and exams. Various features have been included to help you build up your skills and knowledge ready for your assessments.

This book, and the other companion volumes in this series, should help you learn through testing and assessing yourself – it should provide an indication of how advanced your thinking and understanding is. Once you have assessed your understanding you can explore what you need to learn and how. However, hopefully, quite a bit of what you read here you will already have come across and the text will act as a reminder and set your mind at rest – you do know your material.

Succeeding at MCQs

Exams based on MCQs are becoming more and more frequently used in higher education and particularly in psychology. As such you need to know the best strategy for completing such assessments and succeeding. The first thing to note is, if you know the material then the questions will present no problems – so revise and understand your notes and back this up with in-depth review of material presented in textbooks, specialist materials and journal articles. However, once you have done this you need to look at the technique for answering multiple-choice questions and here are some tips for success:

1. Time yourself. The first important thing to note when you are sitting your examination is the time available to you for completing it. If you have, for example, an hour and a half to answer 100 multiple-choice questions this means you have 54 seconds to complete each question. This means that you have to read, interpret, think about and select one answer for a multiple-choice question in under a minute. This may seem impossible, but there are several things that you can do to use your time effectively.

2. Practise. By using the examples in this book, those given out in your courses, in class tests, or on the web you can become familiar with the format and wording of multiple-choice questions similar to those used in your exam. Another way of improving your chances is to set your own multiple-choice exams – try and think of some key questions and your four optional responses (including the correct one of course!). Try and think of optional distractors that are sensible and not completely obvious. You could, of course, swap questions with your peers – getting them to set some questions for you while you set some questions for them. Not only will this help you with your practice but you will also understand the format of MCQs and the principles underlying their construction – this will help you answer the questions when it comes to the real thing.

3. The rule of totality. Look out for words like 'never' and 'always' in multiple-choice questions. It is rare in psychology for any answer to be true in relation to these words of 'totality'. As we all know, psychology is a multi-modal subject that has multiple perspectives and conflicting views and so it is very unlikely that there will always be a 'never' or an 'always'. When you see these words, focus on them and consider them carefully. A caveat is, of course, sometimes never and always will appear in a question, but be careful of these words!

4. Multiple, multiple-choice answers. Some multiple-choice answers will contain statements such as 'both A and C' or 'all of the above' or 'none of these'. Do not be distracted by these choices. Multiple-choice questions have only one correct answer and do not ask for opinion or personal bias. Quickly go through each choice independently, crossing off the answers that you know are not true. If, after eliminating the incorrect responses, you think there is more than one correct answer, group your answers and see if one of the choices matches yours. If you believe only one answer is correct, do not be distracted by multiple-choice possibilities.

5. 'First guess is best' fallacy. There is a myth among those who take (or even write) MCQs that the 'first guess is best'. This piece of folklore is misleading: research (and psychologists love research) indicates that when people change their answers on an MCQ exam, about two-thirds of the time they go from wrong to right, showing that the first guess is often not the best. So, think about it and consider your answer – is it right? Remember, your first guess is not better than a result obtained through good, hard, step-by-step, conscious thinking that enables you to select the answer that you believe to be the best.

6. The rule of threes. One of the most helpful strategies for multiple-choice questions is a three-step process:

(i)   Read the question thoroughly but quickly. Concentrate on particular words such as 'due to' and 'because' or 'as a result of' and on words of totality such as 'never' or 'always' (although see rule 3 above).

(ii) Rather than going to the first answer you think is correct (see rule 5) eliminate the ones that you think are wrong one by one. While this may take more time, it is more likely to provide the correct answer. Furthermore, answer elimination may provide a clue to a misread answer you may have overlooked.

(iii) Reread the question, as if you were reading it for the first time. Now choose your answer from your remaining answers based on this rereading.

7. Examine carefully. Examine each of the questions carefully, particularly those that are very similar. It may be that exploring parts of the question will be useful – circle the parts that are different. It is possible that each of the alternatives will be very familiar and hence you must **understand the meaning** of each of the alternatives with respect to the context of the question. You can achieve this by studying for the test as though it will be a short-answer or essay test. Look for the level of **qualifying words**. Such words as *best, always, all, no, never, none, entirely, completely* suggest that a condition exists without exception. Items containing words that provide for some level of exception or qualification are: *often, usually, less, seldom, few, more* and *most* (and see rule 3). If you know that two or three of the options are correct, **'all of the above'** is a strong possibility.

8. Educated guesses. Never leave a question unanswered. If nothing looks familiar, pick the answer that seems most complete and contains the most information. Most of the time (if not all of the time!) the best way to answer a question is to know the answer! However, there may be times when you will not know the answer or will not really understand the question. There are three circumstances in which you should guess: when you are stuck, when you are running out of time, or both of these! Guessing strategies are always dependent on the scoring system used to mark the exam (see the section on MCQ scoring mechanisms). If the multiple-choice scoring system makes the odds of gaining points equal to the odds of having points deducted it does not pay to guess if you are unable to eliminate any of the answers. But the odds of improving your test score are in your favour if you can rule out even one of the answers. The odds in your favour increase as you rule out more answers in any one question. So, take account of the scoring mechanisms and then eliminate, move onwards and guess!

9. Revise and learn. Study carefully and learn your material. The best tip for success is always to learn the material. Use this book, use your material, use your time wisely but, most of all, use your brain!

Chapter 1
Introduction to
social psychology

This chapter includes questions on the philosophical bases of contemporary social psychology, including mainstream/experimental social psychology, critical social psychology and the subject scope and content for social psychological research.

Select one of the possible answers for each question.

Foundation level questions

1. Which of the following terms best describes the mainstream social psychological approach?

   A. The study of emotions and social connectivity.

   B. The study of cognitions, attitudes and beliefs.

   C. The scientific study of the way in which behaviour is influenced and affected by other people.

   D. The scientific study of individual differences.

   Your answer: ☐

2. Social psychology originally developed from which two approaches?

   A. Behaviourism and Gestalt psychology.

   B. Crowd psychology and *Völkerpsychologie*.

   C. Field theory and modernism.

   D. None of the above.

   Your answer: ☐

3. What distinction between different types of social psychological research did Kurt Lewin propose in the 1940s?

A. Basic and applied.

B. Basic and advanced.

C. Basic and detailed.

D. Exploratory and explanatory.

Your answer:

4. In social psychology, an organised system of ideas that attempts to explain the relationship between events or phenomena is called what?

A. A construct.

B. A directional hypothesis.

C. A non-directional hypothesis.

D. A theory.

Your answer:

5. Which of the following dimensions reflects the differing emphasis placed by some cultures on loyalty, harmony, autonomy and self-sufficiency?

A. Objectivism – interpretivism.

B. Internal focus – external focus.

C. Individualism – collectivism.

D. Flexibility – stability.

Your answer:

6. Which of the following methodologies is less commonly used in social psychological research?

A. Field study.

B. Survey design.

C. True experimental design.

D. Quasi-experimental design.

Your answer:

7. Which of the following lists contains the four main research strategies within social psychology which are based upon different ontological and epistemological foundations?

   A. Inductive, deductive, retroductive, abductive.

   B. Inductive, deductive, retrospective, prospective.

   C. Hypothetical, deductive, inductive, abductive.

   D. Hypothetical, inductive, retroductive, abductive.

Your answer: ☐

8. Which of the following is a criticism of the mainstream social psychology approach often raised by critical social psychologists?

   A. Mainstream social psychology is reductionist, meaning it attempts to explain complex phenomena in simple terms which are not very meaningful.

   B. Mainstream social psychology does not focus enough on the true objective reality and is instead too concerned with subjective realities.

   C. Mainstream social psychological research places too great an emphasis on the individual.

   D. Both A and C.

Your answer: ☐

9. What is the view of social constructionism regarding the concept of knowledge?

   A. There is only one objective reality, knowledge of which can be objectively discovered and documented through careful investigation of social phenomena.

   B. There is no single objective reality, therefore knowledge is created and maintained by social processes.

   C. There is an objective reality but it is heavily masked by social processes. Therefore objective knowledge can only be gained by specifically developed social psychological methodologies designed to overcome this.

   D. There are many social and psychological realities but true knowledge about the social world is only discovered through the use of the scientific method.

Your answer: ☐

10. Social constructionism, postmodernism and discourse analysis are associated with which of the following approaches?

    A. Mainstream social psychology.

    B. Critical social psychology.

    C. Behaviourism.

    D. Social neuroscience.

Your answer: ☐

Advanced level questions

11. Why did psychologists such as Lewin and Sherif rebel against the domination of the behaviourist approach in social psychology in the USA in the 1940s?

    A. They felt that behaviourism was becoming unfashionable.

    B. They felt behaviourism was not suitably rigorous for the type of research they wanted to conduct.

    C. They disagreed with the fact that behaviourism advocated the exclusion of mental states from study, because they could not be objectively observed.

    D. All of the above.

Your answer:

12. Why is mainstream social psychology described as a science?

    A. It uses experiments to investigate social phenomena.

    B. It aims to accumulate facts and knowledge.

    C. It uses the hypothetico-deductive/scientific method to investigate social phenomena.

    D. Both A and C.

Your answer: ☐

13. With which branch of social psychology are concepts such as social roles, cultural norms and socio-economic status most associated?

A. Psychological social psychology.

B. Sociological social psychology.

C. Cognitive social psychology.

D. Social cognitive neuroscience.

Your answer: ☐

14. 'Semiotics' is the study of what?

A. Signs and symbols and how they convey meaning and significance.

B. Process and change.

C. Situated identities.

D. The set of norms people use as a reference point to judge their own.

Your answer: ☐

15. Complete the following sentence:
Psychological social psychology primarily follows the _____, whereas sociological social psychology is associated more strongly with _____ and _____.

A. Experimental approach, naturalistic observation, surveys.

B. Naturalistic observation approach, experiments, surveys.

C. Survey approach, naturalistic observation, experiments.

D. Phenomenological approach, naturalistic observation, experiments.

Your answer: ☐

16. Critical realism and critical relativism are epistemological positions associated with which of the following approaches?

A. Positivism.

B. Rationalism.

C. Modernism.

D. Postmodernism.

Your answer: ☐

17. According to Berger and Luckmann (1967), which of the following contains a list of the three 'moments' through which reality is constructed?

A. Sourcing, objectifying, grounding.

B. Identification, comparison, attribution.

C. Externalisation, objectification, internalisation.

D. Categorisation, experience, interpretation.

Your answer: ☐

18. Complete the following statement:
Experimental social psychology seeks to produce _____ _____, whereas critical social psychology seeks to produce _____ _____.

A. Nomothetic explanations, idiographic explications.

B. Nomothetic explications, idiographic explanations.

C. Unlimited explanations, limited explanations.

D. Complex explanations, simple explications.

Your answer: ☐

19. 'Humaneering' and political activism are examples of the different approaches taken by experimental/mainstream social psychologists and critical social psychologists to what?

A. Attempting to obtain ethical approval for research.

B. Attempting to 'make society a better place'.

C. Attempting to obtain funding.

D. None of the above.

Your answer: ☐

20. In the UK, when did critical social psychology start to become a prominent, recognised approach?

A. The mid-1970s.

B. The mid-1980s.

C. The mid-1990s.

D. The mid-2000s.

Your answer: ☐

Extended multiple-choice question

Complete the following paragraph using the items listed below. Not all of the items will be consistent with the paragraph and not all items can be used. Items can be used only once.

A distinction needs to be made between modernist and postmodernist approaches to social psychology. _____ is based on the assumption that _____ is the only way in which rational knowledge can be gained. However, _____ argues that knowledge is _____ rather than _____ and is _____ rather than _____. Postmodernist proponents argue that knowledge is not ideologically _____ and is in fact a means by which _____ is exercised. It can be seen that _____ social psychology is aligned with modernist principles, whereas _____ social psychology is aligned with postmodernist principles.

Optional items

A. discovered

B. modernism

C. neutral

D. mainstream

E. constructed

F. multiple

G. power

H. singular

I. science

J. biased

K. support

L. postmodernism

M. critical

Essay questions for Chapter 1

Once you have completed the MCQs above you are ready to tackle some essay questions. You might like to select three or four topics and make notes on them. One way of doing this is to create a concept map. The first question has been done for you and you can see how the knowledge required links to some of the MCQs in this chapter.

1. Compare and evaluate the mainstream/experimental social psychological and critical social psychological approaches to understanding social processes and phenomena.

2. 'One cannot study the self without also exploring social processes.' Critically discuss the extent to which you agree with this position, providing evidence from psychological theory and research to support your argument.

3. Critically evaluate the position that social psychology should aim to identify universal laws underpinning behaviour.

4. Critically examine the degree to which 'social psychology' represents a single, unified approach to studying human behaviour. Provide examples of the relevant social psychological theories and research to illustrate your argument.

5. Critically discuss the extent to which you agree with the proposition that we as humans construct our social reality. Illustrate your argument with examples of psychological theories and research.

6. 'Social psychology is merely common sense.' Critically evaluate this position, providing examples of psychological theory and research to illustrate your argument.

7. Critically evaluate the extent to which social psychological research should follow the hypothetico-deductive model of inquiry. Provide examples of relevant research and theory to support your argument.

8. Critically discuss why it is important for social psychologists to adhere to a code of conduct and ethics, such as that published by the British Psychological Society. Consider the implications this has for social psychological research.

Chapter 1 essay question: concept map

Compare and evaluate the mainstream/experimental social psychological and critical social psychological approaches to understanding social processes and phenomena.

The concept map below provides an example of how the first sample essay may be conceptualised. Consideration of the different approaches taken by quantitative and qualitative researchers to exploring psychological processes and phenomena reveals several subtopics. Critically evaluating this provides insight into the emphasis placed on reporting statistics, researcher reflexivity and extant theory, for example. Also revealed are differences in the conceptualisation and method of reporting theory generation. Exploring these issues demonstrates an understanding of the implications that different reporting styles have on understanding psychological and social phenomena.

Remember that it is important to link your answers to other topic areas not covered in this chapter.

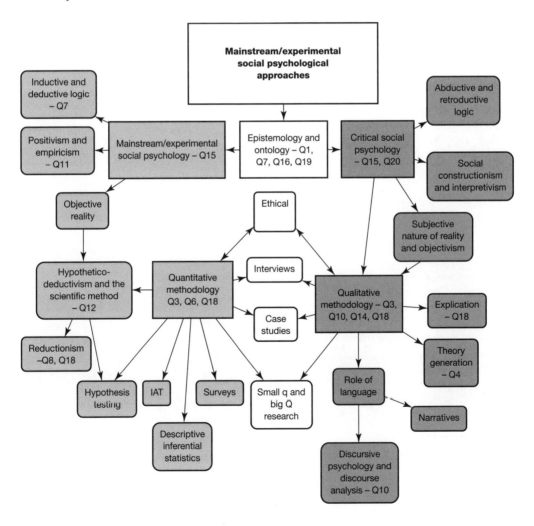

Chapter 2
Understanding social identities

This chapter will cover topics including social identity theory, self-categorisation theory and social comparison theory, self-concept, self-esteem, self-control, self-serving bias and self-presentation.

Select one of the possible answers for each question.

Foundation level questions

1. The 'self' is often defined as a *social* being in social psychological research for what reason?

   A. Because people live in societies.

   B. Because people like to seek out social interaction.

   C. Because the 'self' develops within a social context.

   D. Because otherwise it suggests people are antisocial.

   Your answer:

2. According to G.H. Mead, where does the self originate or emerge from?

   A. Observable behaviour.

   B. Social interaction.

   C. Language.

   D. Social norms.

   Your answer:

3. The process by which children develop beliefs about themselves that are mostly a reflection of the evaluations of other people is known as what?

   A. Self-concept.

   B. Reflected appraisal.

   C. Self-image.

   D. Self-presentation.

   Your answer:

4. According to William James, when a person compares their successes relative to their interests, this is a measure of that person's what?

   A. Self-concept.

   B. Self-presentation.

   C. Self-esteem.

   D. Self-belief.

Your answer: ☐

5. The psychological phenomenon by which an individual becomes an object of attention to themselves is known as what?

   A. Self-concept.

   B. Self-perception.

   C. Self-validation.

   D. Self-awareness.

Your answer: ☐

6. What are the beliefs which contribute to an individual's self-concept called?

   A. Self-schemas.

   B. Social identities.

   C. Self-descriptions.

   D. Self-serving bias.

Your answer: ☐

7. The groups to which an individual belongs contribute to their self-concept. What is this aspect of self-concept known as?

   A. Social identity.

   B. Self-perception.

   C. Individual identity.

   D. Self-enhancement.

Your answer: ☐

8. The goal of controlling what others think of us in order to gain something is an aspect of what?

A. Impression management.

B. Impression formation.

C. Self-esteem.

D. Self-identity.

Your answer:

9. George Herbert Mead was an influential social psychologist who was interested in exploring how self-perception developed. His work into this area became the foundation of which school of social psychology?

A. Social neuroscience.

B. Social constructionism.

C. Symbolic interactionism.

D. Transcendental phenomenology.

Your answer:

10. A participant is asked to write down five sentences beginning with 'I am ...' Taken together what would these five sentences be describing?

A. An individual's self-belief.

B. An individual's self-esteem.

C. An individual's self-efficacy.

D. An individual's self-concept.

Your answer:

Advanced level questions

11. How do the concepts of self-consciousness and self-awareness differ?

    A. Self-consciousness is conceptualised as a relatively stable personality trait whereas self-awareness is a transitory psychological state.

    B. Self-consciousness is conceptualised as a transitory psychological state whereas self-awareness is a relatively stable personality trait.

    C. Self-consciousness is expressed publicly whereas self-awareness is expressed privately.

    D. Self-consciousness is expressed privately whereas self-awareness is expressed publicly.

Your answer:

12. The process of interpreting situations in a positive light to oneself or seeking out situations which confirm this is known as what?

    A. Self-verification.

    B. Self-enhancement.

    C. Self-serving bias.

    D. Self-regulation.

Your answer:

13. When someone else is successful at a task, what determines whether you will engage in social reflection or social comparison?

    A. Degree of self-confidence.

    B. Level of self-esteem.

    C. Degree of relevance of the task to your self-concept.

    D. All of the above.

Your answer:

14. In which of the following scenarios is self-presentation likely to be lowest?

A. On a first date.

B. Being interviewed for a job.

C. A meeting at work.

D. Talking with a friend.

Your answer:

15. The statement 'I did well in that exam because I worked really hard on it, but my classmates did well on it because they were lucky' reflects what?

A. Self-serving bias.

B. Self-presentation.

C. Negativity bias.

D. Self-concept bias.

Your answer:

16. Social learning theory originally developed from which approach?

A. Behaviourism.

B. Gestalt psychology.

C. Crowd psychology.

D. Cognitive psychology.

Your answer:

17. What concept did Yang, Chen, Chen, Ying, Wang, Wang and Kolstad (2010) highlight to explain how the perception of self is influenced by social processes and context?

A. Flexible self-awareness.

B. Elastic self-concept.

C. Elastic self-construal.

D. Flexible self-perception.

Your answer:

18. Complete the following sentences:

Although the following terms are often used interchangeably, they have subtle differences. _____ refers to an individual's belief in their competency and ability to succeed in general or in specific tasks, whereas _____ refers to an individual's general feelings of self-worth and self-value. Although very similar, the concept of _____ refers to an individual's self-assurance which is conveyed through consistency and persistency in their behaviour.

A. Self-esteem, self-confidence, self-efficacy.

B. Self-efficacy, self-confidence, self-esteem.

C. Self-efficacy, self-esteem, self-confidence.

D. Self-confidence, self-esteem, self-efficacy.

Your answer: ☐

19. Which of the following examples of self-esteem threat is most likely to motivate self-esteem maintenance behaviour?

A. Identical career goals between married partners.

B. Brothers with similar abilities.

C. Brothers with very different abilities.

D. Both A and C.

Your answer: ☐

20. Complete the following sentences:

When attempts to improve a situation have repeatedly failed, the result may be the development of _____. This contrasts with _____, which is fostered by repeated successful attempts to exert control over one's situation to improve it.

A. Fear, joy.

B. Learned helplessness, self-determination.

C. Self-awareness, self-perception.

D. Internalised locus of control, externalised locus of control.

Your answer: ☐

Extended multiple-choice question

Complete the following paragraph using the items listed below. Not all of the items will be consistent with the paragraph and not all items can be used. Items can be used only once.

A person's _____ (which is based on social groups to which they belong) should be differentiated from their _____ (relating to an individual's unique and idiosyncratic features which appear unrelated to group membership). Two key theories which explore the mechanisms underpinning social identity are the social identity theory (by _____) and self-categorisation theory (_____). Social identity theory proposes that we form our social identity from the group memberships which are _____ to us. This theory suggests we derive _____ from this social identity, through the derogation of _____. Self-categorisation theory suggests that our group memberships influence our social identity, _____ and _____, through processes such as _____.

Optional items

A. outgroups

B. social identity

C. self-esteem

D. personal identity

E. Tajfel and Turner, 1986

F. important

G. self-concept

H. behaviour

I. conformity

J. Turner, Hogg, Oakes, Reicher and Wetherell (1987)

K. enjoyable

L. internalisation

Essay questions for Chapter 2

Once you have completed the MCQs above you are ready to tackle some essay questions. You might like to select three or four topics and make notes on them. One way of doing this is to create a concept map. The first question has been done for you and you can see how the knowledge required links to some of the MCQs in this chapter.

1. To what extent is a person's sense of 'self' shaped by social and cultural and forces? Support your argument with examples of contemporary psychological research.

2. Critically evaluate the concept of 'identity', providing evidence from psychological theory and research.

3. Critically examine how self-efficacy and self-esteem affect an individual's self-concept.

4. What methods of self-presentation do people engage in and what impact does this have on their self-concept? Critically evaluate both positive and negative aspects of this process.

5. To what extent is a person's sense of 'self' shaped by the groups to which they belong? Critically discuss this issue providing examples of psychological theory and research.

6. Critically examine the concept of social categorisation and the purposes it serves. Discuss the extent to which it is a positive psychological tool.

7. Describe and evaluate the cognitive, affective and behavioural implications of social identification, providing examples of psychological theory and research.

8. Describe and evaluate the mechanisms by which people's social identity changes.

Chapter 2 essay question 1: concept map

To what extent is a person's sense of 'self' shaped by social and cultural forces? Support your argument with examples of contemporary psychological research.

The concept map opposite provides an example of how the first sample essay may be conceptualised. Exploring the ways in which traditional social psychological approaches conceptualise 'self' reveals several subtopics, which can be critically evaluated to provide an understanding of important social and cultural forces at play. Examining alternative approaches, such as critical social, biological, and evolutionary psychology, allows important critiques of the traditional approach to be presented. This provides an insight into contemporary debates in psychological research and demonstrates how different branches with social psychology explain the development of 'self'.

Remember that it is important to link your answers to other topic areas not covered in this chapter.

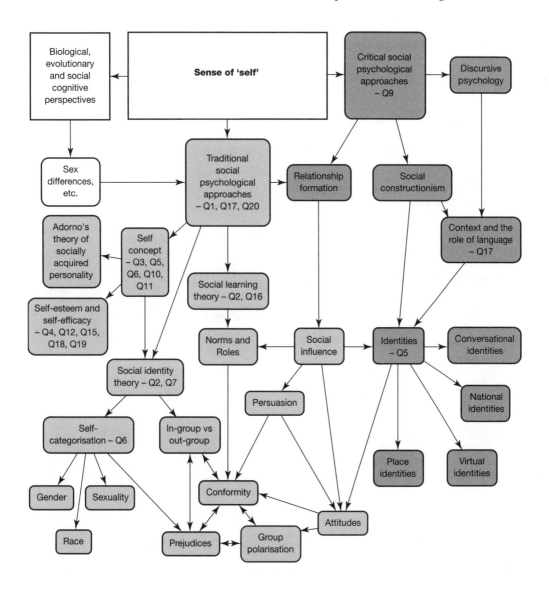

Chapter 3
Making attributions

This chapter contains questions on the key theories of how humans make sense of the world around them, such as social cognition theories and attribution theories, including heuristics, the theory of correspondence inference, fundamental attribution error, actor-observer bias and false consensus effect.

Select one of the possible answers for each question.

Foundation level questions

1. Attribution theory is primarily concerned with which of the following?

    A. The processes by which individuals make judgements about other people's personalities.

    B. The processes by which individuals form impressions of other people's motivations.

    C. The process by which individuals make inferences about the causes of behaviour or events.

    D. The processes by which individuals manage their behaviour in groups.

    Your answer:

2. To what does 'fundamental attribution error' refer?

    A. The tendency to make external attributions for the behaviour of other people.

    B. The tendency to make internal attributions for the behaviour of other people.

    C. The tendency to present only those aspects of the self to other people which are viewed positively.

    D. The tendency to view oneself as more desirable than other people.

    Your answer:

3. Which of the following researchers is most commonly associated with theories about attributional processes?

   A. Fritz Heider.

   B. Hans Eysenck.

   C. Leon Festinger.

   D. Carl Jung.

   Your answer: ☐

4. The need to form a coherent view of the world, to gain control over our environment and to be able to predict what other people will do are all reasons why we do what?

   A. Make attributions.

   B. Form attitudes.

   C. Join groups.

   D. Experience emotions.

   Your answer: ☐

5. What are the two broad categories of information processing called, which reflect the degree of awareness they are associated with?

   A. Involved and uninvolved.

   B. Overt and covert.

   C. Controlled and automatic.

   D. Conscious and unconscious.

   Your answer: ☐

6. What is a 'heuristic'?

   A. A tendency to imagine alternative scenarios to social phenomena that might have happened but did not.

   B. A tendency only to seek out information which confirms a person's thinking.

   C. The perception of uncontrollable events as being within one's control or more controllable than they actually are.

   D. A cognitive strategy and method of problem-solving that enables quick and easy judgements to be made.

   Your answer: ☐

7. Which of the following is a heuristic which bases the belief of the probability of a phenomenon occurring on its accessibility in memory?

A. Representative heuristic.

B. Availability heuristic.

C. Commonplace heuristic.

D. Misperception heuristic.

Your answer:

8. People often perceive the positive actions carried out by the group they belong to as normative and the negative actions as the exception, but tend to view the negative actions carried out by a member of an outgroup as normative and positive actions as the exception. What is this perceptual bias commonly known as?

A. Ultimate attribution error.

B. Ingroup attribution bias.

C. Outgroup attribution bias.

D. Group attribution error.

Your answer:

9. The tendency to believe that our own traits, actions and choices are more common than they actually are is referred to as what?

A. Ultimate attribution error.

B. Hindsight bias.

C. False consensus effect.

D. Counterfactual thinking.

Your answer:

10. Which of the following is not associated with confirmation bias?

A. Cognitive shortcuts.

B. Desire for consensus.

C. High level of self-monitoring.

D. All of the above.

Your answer:

Advanced level questions

11. What are the four main schema types that Fiske and Taylor (1991) suggested people use to help them decide the most appropriate course of action to take, when the requirements of the situation are not obvious?

A. Self, person, role, event.

B. Self, other, event, temporal.

C. Simple, complex, average, vivid.

D. Person, role, temporal, contextual.

Your answer:

12. Your sister tells you that she has lost her job. You think this is probably owing to the fact that her organisation is being forced to downsize. What form of attribution is this?

A. Internal.

B. External.

C. Biased.

D. Dispositional.

Your answer:

13. Lippmann (1922) suggested that in order to be able to cope with the complexity of our social world, we have to create a simpler model to explain and manage it. With which model of social cognition is Lippmann's perspective associated?

A. The naive scientist.

B. The cognitive miser model.

C. The theory of correspondence.

D. The illusory correlation hypothesis.

Your answer:

14. Which of the following theoretical foundations did attribution theory not develop from?

A. Theory of naive psychology.

B. Theory of correspondent inference.

C. The illusory correlation hypothesis.

D. The covariation model.

Your answer:

15. Which of the following types of information did Harold Kelley (1973) suggest we use to make attributions?

A. Consistency.

B. Consensus.

C. Distinctiveness.

D. All of the above.

Your answer:

16. What are the two broad categories of attributions known as?

A. Trait and environmental.

B. Dispositional and situational.

C. Subtle and overt.

D. Simple and complex.

Your answer:

17. The terms *fundamental attribution error* and *correspondence bias* are often used interchangeably, but which of the following statements is most accurate regarding their subtle differences?

    A. Inferences are more automatic than attributional processes, therefore the fundamental attribution error and correspondence bias (based on inferences) require different levels of processing.

    B. Fundamental attribution error results in more negative judgements than correspondence bias.

    C. The fundamental attribution error relates to the tendency to underestimate situational influences and overestimate dispositional influences on other people's behaviour. However, the correspondence bias refers more to the tendency to infer the disposition of a person from what is actually a situational factor.

    D. Both A and C.

Your answer:

18. Nisbett, Caputo, Legant and Marecek (1973) found that when people were asked to tick off statements on a checklist relating to friends' behaviour they chose dispositional items. However, when asked to tick off statements about their own behaviour they tended to choose situational items. Which of the following effects best explains the mechanism underpinning this?

    A. Camera perspective bias.

    B. Actor-observer difference.

    C. False consensus effect.

    D. Just world hypothesis.

Your answer:

19. Which of the following statements is most accurate regarding the fundamental attribution error?

A. Individualist and collectivist cultures both exhibit evidence of the fundamental attribution error.

B. Although there is a great deal of evidence that individualist cultures exhibit the fundamental attribution error, there is little evidence to suggest it occurs in collectivist cultures.

C. Although there is a great deal of evidence to suggest that collectivist cultures exhibit the fundamental attribution error, there is little evidence to suggest it occurs in individualist cultures.

D. No research has been carried out into this topic.

Your answer: ☐

20. Selective recall of past instances of an event (or social phenomena), association between a group and atypical occurrences, and conforming to pre-existing stereotypes are all associated with what?

A. Learned helplessness.

B. Counterfactual thinking.

C. Illusory correlations.

D. Hindsight bias.

Your answer: ☐

Extended multiple-choice question

Complete the following paragraph using the items listed below. Not all of the items will be consistent with the paragraph and not all items can be used. Items can be used only once.

Both the _____ theory and the _____ refer to _____in the way people make attributions. However, they make different suggestions about the way people think; the fundamental attribution error states people have a tendency to attribute the actions of other people to _____. However, the actor-observer effect refers to the fact that an _____ is more likely to make situational attributions regarding a task they are completing, whereas an _____ is more likely to make dispositional attributions about the individual. For example, a student might make the _____ that they are studying for an exam because the _____whereas an observer may make the _____ that the _____.

Optional items

A. the randomness

B. fundamental attribution error

C. dispositional attribution

D. self-presentation

E. biases

F. actor

G. observer

H. actor-observer effect

I. situational attribution

J. exam will be difficult

K. internal dispositions or traits

L. student is a hard worker

Essay questions for Chapter 3

Once you have completed the MCQs above you are ready to tackle some essay questions. You might like to select three or four topics and make notes on them. One way of doing this is to create a concept map. The first question has been done for you and you can see how the knowledge required links to some of the MCQs in this chapter.

1. Critically examine the reasons why people make attributions, providing examples of psychological research to illustrate your answer.

2. Critically discuss the ways in which attribution processes can be 'faulty' and the implications of this, providing examples of psychological theory and research to illustrate your argument.

3. Describe and critically evaluate the cognitive biases which affect the way in which we perceive and understand the social world.

4. Critically examine the role attribution biases play in prejudice, and the methods that could be employed to combat this.

5. Critically evaluate the relationship between controlled and automatic processing of information and the mechanisms underpinning attribution processes.

6. Discuss the roles heuristics play in the way people understand the social world. Provide examples of psychological theory and research to illustrate your answer.

7. Critically evaluate the social and cultural factors which affect the way in which people make attributions, providing examples from contemporary psychological research.

8. Critically compare and evaluate two theories of the attribution process. What do they suggest about the way in which we process information about the world around us?

9. Compare and evaluate the covariation model of attribution and the theory of correspondent inference. Illustrate your argument with examples of relevant psychological theory and research.

Chapter 3 essay question 1: concept map

Critically examine the reasons why people make attributions, providing examples of psychological research to illustrate your answer.

The concept map below provides an example of how the first sample essay may be conceptualised. Consideration of the key concepts identified as important to attribution research in social psychology leads to several subtopics, which must be critically evaluated before conclusions can be drawn. In this case the evidence suggests that a key reason why people make attributions is the need to manage complex information about the world in which they live, and making attributions achieves this by reducing information down (e.g. heuristics, schemas). Understanding how people make attributions, and how these can be flawed (e.g. fundamental attribution error and ultimate attribution error), has implications for psychology's understanding of people's self-concept and identity, group membership, relationship formation, and ultimately prejudice and discrimination.

Remember that it is important to link your answers to other topic areas not covered in this chapter.

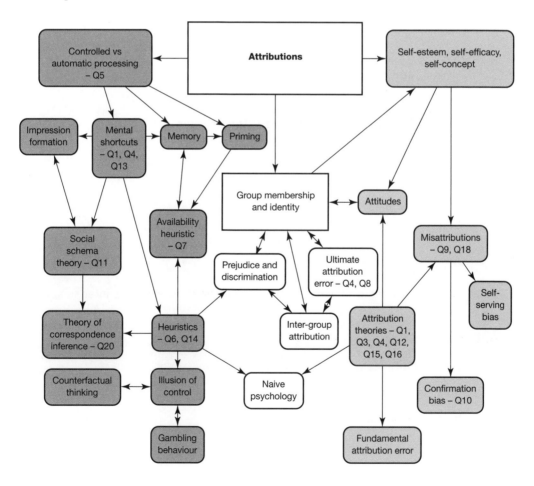

Chapter 4
Attitudes

This chapter contains questions on what attitudes are and how they change, what functions they fulfil, the link between attitude and behaviour, how attitudes are measured and why it is important to study them.

Select one of the possible answers for each question.

Foundation level questions

1. Which of the following theories is an example of an expectancy-value model?

    A. Theory of reasoned action.

    B. The MODE model.

    C. Theory of planned behaviour.

    D. Both A and C.

Your answer:

2. Which of the following is an example of an attitude referent?

    A. An object.

    B. An event.

    C. A person.

    D. All of the above.

Your answer:

3. Which of the following is a term for an argument which is said to be intense and unresponsive to rational argument?

    A. Rational attitude.

    B. Utilitarian attitude.

    C. Symbolic attitude.

    D. Instrumental attitude.

Your answer:

4. Theorists who suggest that attitudes serve to satisfy our psychological needs and therefore will change when our needs change are working from which of the following psychological approaches?

    A. Structural.

    B. Functional.

    C. Cognitive dissonance.

    D. Cognitive consistency.

Your answer:

5. Which of the following are referred to as the 'ABCs' of attitudes?

    A. Action, belief, causation.

    B. Affect, behaviour, cognition.

    C. Altruism, beneficence, conscience.

    D. Action, belief, cognition.

Your answer:

6. Ajzen and Fishbein (1977) proposed which theory concerning the attitude-behaviour link?

    A. Cognitive dissonance.

    B. Cognitive consistency.

    C. Theory of planned behaviour.

    D. The aggregation principle.

Your answer:

7. Models which perceive attitudes as a mental register which individuals consult for the evaluation of the attitude-object, are known as what?

    A. 'File-drawer' models.

    B. Expectancy-value models.

    C. Utilitarian models.

    D. Symbolic function models.

Your answer:

8. If an attitude questionnaire asks people lots of questions which are thought to relate to a particular attitude (i.e. their beliefs and values) but does not explicitly ask about the attitude itself, it is referred to as what?

A. A single-item measure.

B. A direct measure.

C. An indirect measure.

D. An explicit measure.

Your answer: ☐

9. Which of the following is <u>not</u> a form of attitude function?

A. Utilitarian.

B. Value-expressive.

C. Social adjustive.

D. Unpleasantness.

Your answer: ☐

10. At which level of analysis is the study of attitudes important?

A. Individual level.

B. Interpersonal level.

C. Societal level.

D. All of the above.

Your answer: ☐

Advanced level questions

11. What are the four characteristics which Ajzen and Fishbein (1977) suggested can be used to describe both attitudes and behaviours?

A. Correspondence element, aggregation element, consistency and accessibility.

B. Measurement element, moderation element, individual differences element and situational element.

C. Action element, target element, context element and time component.

D. Indirect element, direct element, implicit element, explicit element.

Your answer:

12. In 1969 social psychologist Alan Wicker (1969) reviewed numerous research studies concerning attitudes and behaviour. What did he conclude?

A. Expressed attitudes were poor predictors of behaviour.

B. Expressed attitudes were strong predictors of behaviour.

C. Expressed attitudes were moderate predictors of behaviour.

D. Expressed attitudes were strong predictors of behaviour if the attitude was positive in nature.

Your answer:

13. Intra-attitudinal consistency, accessibility and cognitive effort in attitude formation are all indicators of what?

A. Attitude reliability.

B. Attitude direction.

C. Attitude strength.

D. Attitude complexity.

Your answer:

14. A woman opposes discrimination in the workplace because it violates her sense of social justice and equal opportunities. What type of attitude-function is this an example of?

A. Utilitarian.

B. Value-expressive.

C. Social adjustive.

D. None of the above.

Your answer:

15. Complete the following sentence:
Attitudes and attitude _____ are central features of social psychological research because they are an important _____ on social _____.

A. Traits, control, behaviour.

B. Change, control, presence.

C. Traits, influence, presence.

D. Change, influence, behaviour.

Your answer:

16. Which of the following statements is not true of attitudes formed via the peripheral route of persuasion?

A. They are based only on the processing of relevant factors.

B. They are less accurate in predicting actual behaviour.

C. They are weaker.

D. They are more vulnerable to counter-argument.

Your answer:

17. Which of the following is a key concern with single-item measures of attitudes?

A. Their reliability may be low or difficult to assess.

B. They cannot be used to assess attitude accessibility.

C. They are not economical in research.

D. None of the above.

Your answer:

18. An experiment, such as that used by Greenwald, McGhee and Schwartz (1998), which measures the differential association of two target concepts (e.g. birds vs insects), with positive vs negative evaluations (e.g. pleasant words vs unpleasant words) is known as what?

    A. A multi-item measure.

    B. A priming procedure.

    C. An implicit association test (IAT).

    D. None of the above.

Your answer:

19. To what does the term 'insufficient justification effect' refer?

    A. When participants don't feel there is sufficient justification to explicitly state their attitudes toward an object.

    B. When an individual reduces dissonance by internally justifying their behaviour when external justification is 'insufficient'.

    C. When a person's attitude has insufficient basis in fact for it to be maintained.

    D. When an individual is not sufficiently aware of their own attitude to be able to report it in research.

Your answer:

20. An individual is unsure how they feel about an attitude they hold. According to the self-perception theory of attitudes, what would this individual do?

    A. Infer their attitude from looking at their own behaviour and the circumstances under which it occurs.

    B. Think about what would make them look better to other people and alter their attitude to bring it in line with this.

    C. Compare themselves with people they think they are similar to and adopt their attitudes.

    D. Think about other attitudes they hold to similar attitude-objects to understand their 'average' attitude and infer this particular attitude from this.

Your answer:

Extended multiple-choice question

Using the items listed below complete the following diagram of the Theory of Reasoned Action (TRA) proposed by Fishbein and Ajzen (1975), and then choose all those statements which can be correctly applied to the model it represents.

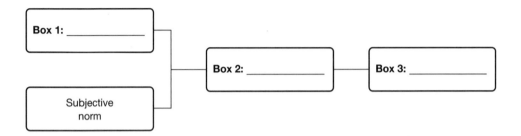

Box 1: _____

Subjective norm

Box 2: _____

Box 3: _____

Optional items

A. Attitude toward the behaviour is defined as the sum of intention × behavioural products.

B. Attitude toward the behaviour.

C. This is an example of an expectancy-value model.

D. Intention.

E. The model was later modified to include 'perceived behavioural control'.

F. Behaviour.

G. The adapted model became known as the 'theory of planned behaviour'.

H. Attitude toward the behaviour is defined as the sum of expectancy × value products.

I. The model was later modified by the authors to include 'attitude valence'.

J. The adapted model became known as the 'cognitive consistency' model.

K. This is an example of a file-drawer model.

L. Cognitive effort.

Essay questions for Chapter 4

Once you have completed the MCQs above you are ready to tackle some essay questions. You might like to select three or four topics and make notes on them. One way of doing this is to create a concept map. The first question has been done for you and you can see how the knowledge required links to some of the MCQs in this chapter.

1. How well do attitudes predict behaviour? Explain your answer with reference to psychological theory and research.

2. Describe and evaluate the ways in which a person's behaviour might affect their attitudes. Provide examples of relevant theory and research to illustrate your arguments.

3. Critically discuss why the study of attitudes is important for organisations undertaking market research.

4. 'Attitudes should only be measured using the indirect approach.' Critically examine this position, providing evidence from research to support your conclusions.

5. Describe and evaluate the issues which psychologists should be aware of when researching attitudes.

6. Describe and discuss the factors which may affect the measurement of attitudes and how they can be overcome.

7. Compare and evaluate two methods of measuring attitudes. Provide examples of psychological research to illustrate their strengths and weaknesses.

8. What ethical considerations do psychologists face when studying attitudes and how can these be overcome?

Chapter 4 essay question 1: concept map

How well do attitudes predict behaviour? Explain your answer with reference to psychological theory and research.

The concept map below provides an example of how the first sample essay may be conceptualised. Consideration of the way attitudes are defined and conceptualised, the different theories of the link between attitudes and behaviour, and the methods of assessing the predictive power of are crucial to understanding this issue. Investigating the further subtopics revealed also highlights important issues such as ethics in attitude–behaviour research and also that certain theories propose that behaviour may actually predict attitudes. Finally examining limitations of research methodology adopted (as this has an impact how the link between attitudes and behaviour can be explored and understood) will provide a full answer to the question posed.

Remember that it is important to link your answers to other topic areas not covered in this chapter.

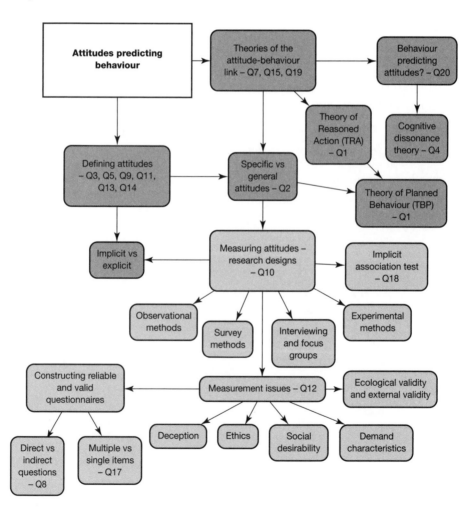

Chapter 5
Social influence

This chapter contains questions on persuasion, including: routes to persuasion, the communicator, the message content and target variables, and resisting persuasion. Aspects of conformity, obedience and majority and minority influence and normalisation are also explored.

Select one of the possible answers for each question.

Foundation level questions

1. When a person is influenced by irrelevant cues rather than careful consideration of an issue, which route to persuasion is being used?

   A. The central route to persuasion.

   B. The cognitive route to persuasion.

   C. The peripheral route to persuasion.

   D. None of the above.

   Your answer:

2. Which researcher used an optical illusion produced by the autokinetic phenomenon to explore norm formation?

   A. Zimbardo.

   B. Sherif.

   C. Asch.

   D. Provine.

   Your answer:

3. Which of the following is not a message variable?

    A. Repetition.

    B. Order of presentation of arguments.

    C. Use of vivid images versus facts.

    D. Credibility.

Your answer:

4. In which of the following situations is evidence immediately more persuasive than the use of vivid images?

    A. When the message is attributed to a very credible source.

    B. When the message combines evidence with peripheral cues.

    C. When the message is delivered by a likeable communicator.

    D. When the message is delivered in a way that enhances the primacy effect.

Your answer: ☐

5. In which of the following situations are fear appeals not effective?

    A. When the audience believes they are capable of taking the action suggested to avoid the danger.

    B. When the audience believes they have no control over the danger.

    C. When the audience believes the probability of the 'danger' occurring is high.

    D. When the audience believes in the seriousness of the danger.

Your answer: ☐

6. Conformity based on a desire to fulfil other people's expectations, usually to gain acceptance, is known as what?

    A. Normative influence.

    B. Informational influence.

    C. Situational influence.

    D. Personal influence.

Your answer: ☐

7. The repetition of a persuasive message is more effective when:

    A. The attitude object is viewed as negative.

    B. The attitude object is viewed as neutral.

    C. The attitude object is viewed as positive.

    D. Both B and C.

Your answer:

8. Which of the following options is *not* a concept comprising conformity?

    A. Compliance.

    B. Obedience.

    C. Acceptance.

    D. None of the above.

Your answer:

9. Which of the following is the key factor affecting whether the primacy effect or recency effect will be more influential?

    A. The speed with which the message is delivered.

    B. Whether a one-sided or two-sided argument is used.

    C. The amount of time elapsed between the message and the making of a decision.

    D. The strength of the argument presented.

Your answer:

10. Which of the following statements regarding role-playing is true?

    A. By intentionally playing a new role and conforming to its expectations, people sometimes change themselves to empathise with people who have different roles to themselves.

    B. Different social roles are associated with conformity to different expectations.

    C. In role-playing you automatically begin to take on the new role's characteristics and conform to new norms.

    D. Both A and C.

Your answer:

Advanced level questions

11. In which situation are the characteristics of the communicator of a message more important for persuasion to be effective?

A. When the message is complex.

B. When the audience is well informed about an issue.

C. When the peripheral route to persuasion is taken.

D. When the central route to persuasion is taken.

Your answer:

12. Which of the following statements most accurately describes the 'sleeper effect'?

A. The finding that a persuasive message from a source low in credibility increases in its effectiveness over time.

B. The finding that a persuasive message from a source high in credibility decreases in its effectiveness over time.

C. The finding that more complex persuasive messages increase in effectiveness with a greater period of exposure.

D. The finding that more complex persuasive messages decrease in effectiveness with a greater period of exposure.

Your answer:

13. In which of the following situations would a two-sided presentation of an argument *not* be more effective?

A. When the audience is well informed about the topic.

B. When the audience disagrees with the communicator.

C. When the recipients will be exposed to differing viewpoints at a later time.

D. When the audience is not paying that much attention.

Your answer:

14. Complete the following sentence using the options provided:

The _____ approach to persuasion is based on the presentation of _____ counter-arguments to the central argument, which are consistently _____, which leads to _____.

A. Inoculation, weaker, supported, strengthening.

B. Vaccination, stronger, refuted, strengthening.

C. Inoculation, weaker, refuted, resistance.

D. Vaccination, stronger, supported, resistance.

Your answer:

15. A cognitive-response explanation suggests that people in a good mood are easier to persuade for what reason?

A. Because they associate the good mood with the persuasive message.

B. Because they are more likely to find the argument rewarding and will want to hear more of it.

C. Because they want to keep their attitudes consistent with their positive mood.

D. Because they are less likely to engage in extensive processing of the argument if their mood is positive.

Your answer:

16. Which of the following individual-differences variables is associated with a greater susceptibility to persuasion?

A. Having a lower need for cognition.

B. Having a lower IQ level.

C. Being a high self-monitor.

D. Both A and C.

Your answer:

17. Which of the following characteristics is not a way in which the communicator of a message may be viewed as attractive to an audience?

A. Appealing physical appearance.

B. Appearing likeable.

C. Appearing knowledgeable about the topic.

D. Appearing similar to the audience.

Your answer:

18. In which situations is humour more likely to increase an audience's attention to and comprehension of a persuasive message?

A. If the humour used is extremely funny.

B. If the humour is directly relevant to the target.

C. If the message refers to something well liked by the audience.

D. If the communicator also employs discounting cues.

Your answer:

19. Which of the following statements is correct?

A. Global personality scores are poor predictors of specific acts of conformity but better at predicting average conformity.

B. Personality traits are better predictors of conformity when social influences are weak.

C. Different cultures are associated with different degrees of conformity.

D. All of the above.

Your answer:

20. In which of the following situations is conformity reduced?

A. If the modelled behaviour or belief is not unanimous.

B. If the status of those modelling the behaviour or belief is high.

C. If a group is not cohesive.

D. Both A and C.

Your answer:

Extented multiple-choice question

Complete the following paragraph using the items listed below and overleaf. Not all of the items will be consistent with the paragraph and not all items can be used. Items can be used only once.

Cults represent important _____ to study in social psychology because they represent examples of extreme persuasion. Cults typically share three characteristics which facilitate this persuasion. Firstly, they involve members making commitments to the cult _____ and repeatedly, a mechanism by which behaviour influences attitudes through the _____ of the commitments. Secondly, they involve '_____': isolating members from their external ties so they only have contact with other like-minded individuals. This isolation leads to a loss of _____, increased group _____ and consensus and ultimately this sense of collective identity leads to increased _____. Cult leaders often apply the principles of _____ persuasion: appearing _____ and charismatic, using varied, _____ and emotional forms of communication and deliberately targeting individuals who may be more vulnerable to their persuasion efforts (for example, targeting people under the age of 25 whose values and attitudes are still developing). It is important to recognise that, despite all these factors, cults do not automatically recruit people and their efforts of persuasion can be resisted through techniques such as _____.

Optional items

A. publicly

B. stress inoculation

C. privately

D. internalisation

E. social implosion

F. counter-arguments

G. cohesion

H. conformity

I. effective

J. groups

K. attitude inoculation

L. credible

M. vivid

N. social explosion

Essay questions for Chapter 5

Once you have completed the MCQs above you are ready to tackle some essay questions. You might like to select three or four topics and make notes on them. One way of doing this is to create a concept map. The first question has been done for you and you can see how the knowledge required links to some of the MCQs in this chapter.

1. 'If put in the right situation, people will do anything they are told.' To what extent do you agree with this statement? Provide examples of psychological research and theory to support your argument.

2. Critically evaluate the mechanisms by which majority and minority influence occur. In what ways are they similar and how do they differ?

3. Describe and evaluate the mechanisms by which persuasion occurs. Discuss the situations in which persuasion is most effective.

4. Compare and critically evaluate two theories of persuasion. Provide examples of relevant research to illustrate their strengths and weaknesses.

5. Critically examine the potential ethical implications of studying conformity under laboratory experiment conditions. How might these concerns be mitigated?

6. Critically examine the factors which affect conformity and how these factors can be ameliorated.

7. Critically discuss the role that group membership plays in forming social norms, social roles and the degree of conformity exhibited by individuals.

8. A psychologist is asked to design a TV advertising campaign aimed at encouraging young adults to drink alcohol responsibly. Utilising your knowledge of persuasion research, critically evaluate the factors that the psychologist should consider, to ensure the campaign is as effective as possible.

Chapter 5 essay question 1: concept map

'If put into the right situation, people will do anything they are told'. To what extent do you agree with this statement? Provide examples of psychological research and theory to support your argument.

The concept map below provides an example of how the first sample essay may be conceptualised. Consideration of the key themes highlighted by research (conformity, persuasion and obedience) reveals several subtopics, which need to be critically evaluated before conclusions can be drawn. In this case the evidence suggests that a combination of factors influences the degree to which individuals will 'do what they are told' and there are plenty of examples from research (e.g. Milgram's research) and contemporary issues (e.g. cults) which can be explored to fully understand the issue.

Remember that it is important to link your answers to other topic areas not covered in this chapter.

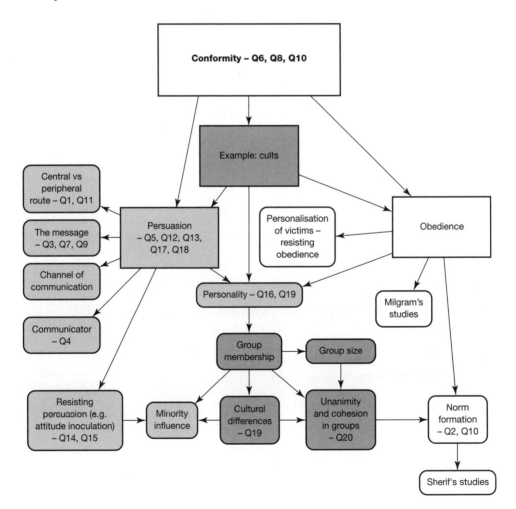

Chapter 6
Group processes

This chapter covers issues concerning defining groups and studying group processes, including phenomena such as audience effects, evaluation apprehension, social facilitation, social loafing, group polarisation, Groupthink, de-individuation and intergroup conflict.

Select one of the possible answers for each question.

Foundation level questions

1. Which of the following is a definition of a 'group' as used in social psychological research?

   A. Groups are defined in terms of a common experience.

   B. Groups are defined in terms of an implicit social structure.

   C. Groups are defined in terms of a mutual dependence between individuals.

   D. All of the above.

   Your answer: ☐

2. Which of the following is not a symptom of Groupthink?

   A. Ignoring warning signs because the group is overly confident in the success of their decisions.

   B. Heightened awareness of ethical issues in decision-making.

   C. Discounting challenges and engaging in self-censorship to maintain the group's cohesion.

   D. Appointing 'Mindguards' who protect the group from information which could lead to decisions being questioned.

   Your answer: ☐

3. Which of the following factors affects group cohesion?

   A. Similarity or diversity of group members.

   B. Group size.

   C. The prestige, or attractiveness of the group.

   D. All of the above.

Your answer: ☐

4. When applied to the study of group processes, to what does the term 'interdependent' refer?

   A. The phenomenon that groups are more likely to form in interdependent cultures.

   B. Groups are based on interaction between group members, making them interdependent.

   C. Events that affect one group member also affect other group members.

   D. All of the above are examples of interdependence.

Your answer: ☐

5. Which of the following has been proposed as an example of the Groupthink phenomenon by psychologists?

   A. The Northern Rock financial crisis (2007).

   B. The invasion of the Bay of Pigs in Cuba, by the Kennedy administration (1961).

   C. The Japanese attack on Pearl Harbour in 1941.

   D. All of the above.

Your answer: ☐

6. What can arousal, diffused responsibility and anonymity result in?

   A. Social facilitation.

   B. De-individuation.

   C. Groupthink.

   D. Risky shift phenomena.

Your answer: ☐

7. Which form of group decision-making rule tends to result in the greatest amount of group member satisfaction?

   A. Compromise.

   B. Plurality.

   C. Majority.

   D. Unanimity.

Your answer:

8. To what does 'group polarisation' refer?

   A. When groups intensify opinions.

   B. When groups lead to more risky decisions.

   C. When groups become fractured and splinter apart.

   D. When groups become very unstable.

Your answer:

9. Social loafing is most often attributed to what?

   A. Confusion over task goals.

   B. Differences in opinions between group members.

   C. Loss of motivation.

   D. Loss of concentration.

Your answer:

10. Stoner (1961) proposed which theory that later became the foundation of the group polarisation concept?

   A. Risky shift phenomenon.

   B. Equity in effort theory.

   C. Evaluation apprehension theory.

   D. Social compensation theory.

Your answer:

Advanced level questions

11. The theory that group members will deliberately exert less effort on a task because they believe other members are deliberately withholding effort on a task, is known as what?

A. Social loafing.

B. Equity in effort.

C. The sucker effect.

D. Social labouring.

Your answer:

12. Holt (1987) argued that when group membership is important to an individual they will exhibit greater effort on a task. He therefore proposed that the social loafing concept be revised and divided into two new concepts, which he called what?

A. Individual loafing, social labouring.

B. Individual loafing, social compensation.

C. Social loafing, individual labouring.

D. Social loafing, individual compensation.

Your answer:

13. What is the main difference between situations that elicit increased performance on a task through social facilitation and those that encourage social loafing?

A. Social facilitation is more likely to occur in groups where people know each other whereas social loafing occurs with groups of strangers.

B. Social facilitation is more likely to occur in large groups whereas social loafing is more likely to occur in small groups.

C. Social facilitation effects typically occur when an individual's unique contribution to a task is witnessed by an audience whereas social loafing typically occurs when individuals are acting together as part of a group.

D. Social facilitation effects occur regardless of culture whereas social loafing only occurs in collectivist cultures.

Your answer:

14. Steiner (1972) suggested that most group deficit theories typically base their conceptualisation of group productivity on which of the following models?

    A. Actual performance = potential performance – losses due to faulty processes.

    B. Potential performance = actual performance – losses due to faulty processes.

    C. Actual performance = potential performance – loss of motivation.

    D. Actual performance = expected performance – losses due to faulty processes.

Your answer: ☐

15. Group membership can result in de-individuation. Which of the following forms of behaviour may be promoted by this?

    A. Enhanced performance on tasks.

    B. Social loafing.

    C. Risky shift in judgements.

    D. Antisocial behaviour.

Your answer: ☐

16. In which situations does group polarisation typically occur?

    A. Group polarisation can occur when there is discussion between like-minded individuals, and opinions held by the group can become more extreme.

    B. Group polarisation may occur as a result of social comparison, where people evaluate their opinions and abilities against those of other group members. To encourage other people to like them group members may express more similar views more strongly.

    C. Group polarisation may arise as a result of normative influence, resulting from cultural values evoked by contextual information.

    D. All of the above.

Your answer: ☐

17. Ng and Van Dyne (2001) found that the effect of majority and minority influence may be different for different types of culture. Specifically, their findings suggested what?

A. Group members who value collectivist beliefs are more likely to be influenced by the majority rather than the minority.

B. Group members who value collectivist beliefs are more likely to be influenced by the minority rather than the majority.

C. Group members from individualist cultures are more likely to be influenced by the majority rather than the minority.

D. Both A and C.

Your answer:

18. An organisation needs assembly workers to produce large numbers of packaging for dairy products. This is a straightforward task but repetitive. According to the social facilitation theory proposed by Zajonc (1965), how should the company organise their workforce, to encourage optimal performance?

A. Each assembly worker should work in a separate room in isolation.

B. Assembly workers should all work together in the same room.

C. It is not possible to say until the specific conditions of this particular organisation have first been examined.

D. Whether the assembly workers work in the same room or in isolation will have little effect on their performance.

Your answer:

19. What recommendations did Janis (1982) make to combat Groupthink?

A. Appointing a 'devil's advocate' to encourage critical evaluation and impartiality.

B. Dividing a group into smaller units to work or generate ideas on a task, then reuniting these subgroups to encourage discussion and generation of ideas about the task.

C. Ensuring advice from appropriate external sources is sought and 'second chance' meetings are held to ensure all group members have an opportunity to voice and discuss concerns.

D. All of the above.

Your answer:

20. Which of the following statements is incorrect?

A. Social loafing does not occur within groups where members know each other.

B. Social loafing is less likely to occur if group membership or the group's goals are important to an individual.

C. Social loafing may be mediated by the level of perceived effort of other group members.

D. The perception of a group member as engaging in social loafing can lead other group members to engage in socially destructive behaviours (e.g. ostracism).

Your answer: ☐

Extended multiple-choice question

Complete the following paragraph using the items listed below and opposite. Not all of the items will be consistent with the paragraph and not all items can be used. Items can be used only once.

In 1898 Triplett conducted one of the first ever _____ experiments in social psychology. He asked children, either on their own or among a group of other children, to _____ as fast as they could. Triplett found that children who performed the task among other children were _____ (an example of an _____). He therefore suggested that the mere presence of other people is enough to enhance task performance, an effect he called _____. However, other research found the opposite could also be true. Therefore in 1965 _____ modified the theory to suggest that the presence of other people results in _____, which will lead to the enhancement of the _____. Therefore, in a simple task, the social facilitation effect will result in greater confidence and increased performance, but in a complex task this will result in greater anxiety and a decrease in performance.

Optional items

A. Zajonc

B. a motivation effect

C. laboratory

D. wind string on a reel

E. quicker

F. evaluation apprehension

G. slower

H. an audience effect

I. social facilitation

J. complete a finger maze

K. Eysenck

L. dominant response tendency

Essay questions for Chapter 6

Once you have completed the MCQs above you are ready to tackle some essay questions. You might like to select three or four topics and make notes on them. One way of doing this is to create a concept map. The first question has been done for you and you can see how the knowledge required links to some of the MCQs in this chapter.

1. Why is it important to study group processes in social psychology? Discuss, providing examples of social psychological theory and research.

2. From social psychological theories of group processes, critically discuss why it may be difficult to change the organisational culture of a team which is not performing effectively.

3. Whyte (1989) argued that Groupthink is not actually a unitary phenomenon, but is a collection of social psychological phenomena already documented by other psychologists. Critically debate this position, providing relevant examples of research to support your argument.

4. Describe and evaluate the positive and negative aspects of cohesive groups and why it is important to understand them.

5. Discuss the processes groups use to reach decisions. How can they be improved to encourage effective decision-making?

6. What are social dilemmas and why do they occur? Compare and evaluate two methods that can be adopted to reduce them.

7. 'Decision-making is always hindered by group processes.' Discuss this statement with reference to relevant social psychological theory and research.

8. 'Groups are always less productive than individuals.' Discuss this statement with reference to relevant social psychological theory and research.

Chapter 6 essay question 1: concept map

Why is it important to study group processes in social psychology? Discuss, providing examples of psychological theory and research.

The concept map below provides an example of how the first sample essay may be conceptualised. Consideration of the key topics in group process research (e.g., decision-making and productivity, social influence and self-concept) introduces numerous subtopics. Critically exploring these issues reveals the wide-ranging implications group processes have for our understanding of concepts such as prejudice, discrimination and relationship formation, and will provide a full answer to the question posed.

Remember that it is important to link your answers to other topic areas not covered in this chapter.

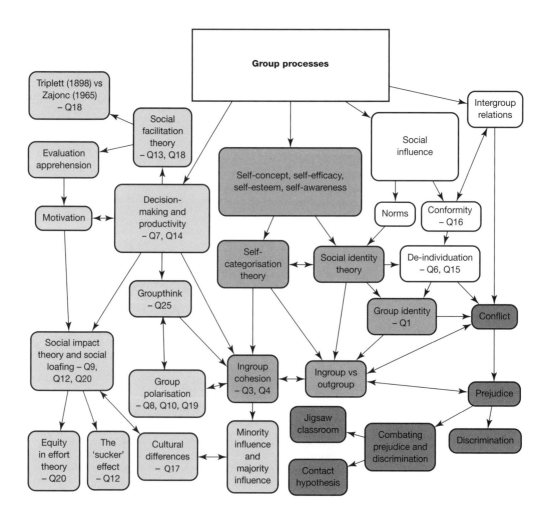

Chapter 7
Prejudice

This chapter covers questions on the meaning of prejudice, stereotyping and discrimination, the sources of prejudice, the role motivation and cognition play in prejudice, the consequences of prejudice and how prejudice can be tackled.

Select one of the possible answers for each question.

Foundation level questions

1. What does the term 'prejudice' refer to?

    A. Hostility towards another person.

    B. Negative attitudes towards a group and its members without basis in fact.

    C. Differences assumed to exist between groups of people.

    D. Preconceptions about another person's personality.

Your answer: ☐

2. A university lecturer assumes that the younger students in his class will struggle academically compared to the mature students. Which of the following is this an example of?

    A. Discrimination.

    B. Prejudice.

    C. Stereotyping.

    D. Homogeneity bias.

Your answer: ☐

3. Which of the following is not an aspect of realistic group conflict theory?

A. Stereotype threat.

B. Competition for rare resources.

C. Increasing hostility towards outgroup members.

D. Increase in ethnocentrism.

Your answer:

4. What did the classic study carried out by Sherif, called the 'Robbers' cave' study, explore?

A. Realistic group conflict theory.

B. Contact hypothesis.

C. Social comparison theory.

D. Social identity theory.

Your answer:

5. A Sikh man is told by his employer that he is not allowed to wear headwear because it is not part of the uniform that all employees must wear. What form of discrimination is this an example of?

A. Direct discrimination.

B. Indirect discrimination.

C. Moderate discrimination.

D. This example does not demonstrate any form of discrimination.

Your answer:

6. What is the tendency to give more favourable evaluations and rewards to members of a group to which you belong called?

A. Outgroup homogeneity bias.

B. Ethnocentrism.

C. Ingroup bias.

D. Contact hypothesis.

Your answer:

7. Which of the following is not an example of an ascribed status?

    A. Sexual orientation.

    B. Gender.

    C. Race.

    D. Religious orientation.

Your answer: ☐

8. Which of the following researchers argues that our tendency to stereotype is a feature of our biological heritage?

    A. Henri Tajfel.

    B. Else Frenkel-Brunswik.

    C. Robin Fox.

    D. Muzafer Sherif.

Your answer: ☐

9. For which of the following could the contact hypothesis serve as a framework?

    A. Reducing a person's tendency to stereotype members of outgroups.

    B. Reducing the degree of hostility between groups with a history of conflict.

    C. Reducing discrepancies between different groups' statuses.

    D. Increasing self-esteem of members of an ingroup.

Your answer: ☐

10. What are the two main forms of prejudice?

    A. Justified and unjustified.

    B. Subtle and overt.

    C. Discriminatory and non-discriminatory.

    D. Generalised and specific.

Your answer: ☐

Advanced level questions

11. An individual is most likely to experience 'stereotype threat' if they have what?

    A. Never experienced discrimination before.

    B. Often experienced discrimination.

    C. No access, or limited access, to social support systems.

    D. Both A and C.

    Your answer:

12. Henri Tajfel proposed that the existence of two groups was the minimal requirement for what?

    A. Social comparison.

    B. Social categorisation.

    C. Ethnocentrism.

    D. Competition.

    Your answer:

13. When members of a minority group compare themselves to the majority on attributions which are central to their social identity, what may be reversed?

    A. Ingroup homogeneity effect.

    B. Outgroup homogeneity effect.

    C. Ingroup bias.

    D. Outgroup bias.

    Your answer:

14. What is Aronson's 'jigsaw classroom' primarily an example of?

    A. A cooperative learning technique used to reduce intergroup tension.

    B. A method of combating authoritarian personalities.

    C. A cooperative learning technique used to reduce intragroup tension.

    D. A method of reducing institutional discrimination.

    Your answer:

15. In the intermediate stages of the 'Robbers' Cave' study increasing loyalty within the ingroup and increasing hostility toward the outgroup were observed. What is this an example of?

    A. Stereotypic thinking.

    B. Ethnocentrism.

    C. Oppositional identity.

    D. Social comparison effect.

Your answer:

16. Individuals high in social dominance orientation tend to what?

    A. View people in terms of hierarchies.

    B. Be high in self-esteem.

    C. Be motivated to have their group dominate other social groups.

    D. Both A and C.

Your answer:

17. Categorisation, identification and comparison are central themes in which of the following theories concerned with the motivational sources of prejudice?

    A. Social identity theory.

    B. The realistic group conflict theory.

    C. The scapegoat theory.

    D. Both A and C.

Your answer:

18. Which of the following statements regarding the cognitive sources of prejudice is true?

   A. Stereotypic thinking reflects the way people attempt to understand the world around them through simplifying it.

   B. The distinctiveness of people and events makes people aware of differences that would otherwise be unnoticed. If two such distinctive events co-occur, they appear linked. That is, there is an illusory correlation between them which can lead to faulty attributions and prejudice.

   C. People often believe in a just world (i.e. people get what they deserve); this leads to faulty attributions and can lead to prejudice.

   D. All of the above.

Your answer:

19. When information becomes apparent which drastically deviates from a stereotype held by a person, what are the most likely methods by which that person will deal with it?

   A. By accommodating the individual who deviates from the stereotype in a new subgroup of the stereotype (subgrouping).

   B. By discounting their stereotype.

   C. By viewing the individual who deviates from the stereotype by viewing them as an exception (subtyping).

   D. Both A and C.

Your answer:

20. In what ways do stereotypes bias the way people make judgements about others?

   A. People often evaluate individuals more positively than the groups they compose.

   B. People will often ignore the stereotypes they hold if they are presented with personalised, anecdotal information about a person.

   C. Strong and relevant stereotypes are much more likely to affect our judgements of individuals.

   D. All of the above.

Your answer:

Extended multiple-choice question

Complete the following paragraph using the items listed below. Not all of the items will be consistent with the paragraph and not all items can be used. Items can be used only once.

There are two main types of prejudice, which are known as subtle (largely _____) and overt (_____). These two different types of prejudice require different methods to measure and detect them. For example, to detect subtle prejudice researchers have needed to develop _____ and _____ measures, such as the _____. There is evidence to suggest that although explicit attitudes may change dramatically through _____, implicit attitudes are more resistant and may only change through _____ and _____. There is also evidence to suggest that different areas of the brain are implicated in automatic prejudice and conscious prejudice: the _____ (a primitive region of the brain associated with fear) is associated with unconscious prejudice, whereas the _____ (which is associated with conscious thinking) is associated with more conscious prejudice.

Optional items

A. education

B. unconscious

C. implicit association test (IAT)

D. discrete survey questions

E. indirect

F. conscious

G. amygdala

H. direct

I. unstructured interview

J. new habits

K. practice

L. frontal cortex

Essay questions for Chapter 7

Once you have completed the MCQs above you are ready to tackle some essay questions. You might like to select three or four topics and make notes on them. One way of doing this is to create a concept map. The first question has been done for you and you can see how the knowledge required links to some of the MCQs in this chapter.

1. Describe and evaluate the concepts of subtle and overt prejudice. What are their implications and how can they be overcome? Provide evidence to support your argument.

2. Describe and evaluate two different methods of combating prejudice and discrimination. Providing evidence from psychological theory and research discuss which method you believe is the most effective.

3. Describe and evaluate the social, motivational and cognitive sources of prejudice and the methods which can be used to overcome them.

4. Critically discuss the role that stereotypes play in prejudice and discrimination. Provide examples of contemporary social psychological research to illustrate your answer.

5. Critically examine the difficulties psychologists encounter when studying prejudice. Provide examples of how these difficulties have been overcome in contemporary psychological research.

6. Describe and discuss the consequences of prejudice and discrimination, considering the issues at both the individual and societal level.

7. Compare and evaluate personality, cognitive and discursive accounts of prejudice, providing examples of research and theory to illustrate their strengths and weaknesses.

8. Prejudiced stereotypes are often directed toward low-status groups in society. Discuss why this is the case, what the potential consequences of this are and how this can be combated.

Chapter 7 essay question 1: concept map

Describe and evaluate the concepts of subtle and overt prejudice. What are their implications and how can they be overcome? Provide evidence to support your argument.

The concept map below provides an example of how the first sample essay may be conceptualised. Exploring the differences between subtle and overt prejudice leads to several subtopics, such as how they are manifested, how they can be measured and ultimately how they can be understood. Critically discussing these issues also highlights the methodological and ethical considerations that come into play when researching prejudice and discrimination, and the strategies researchers adopt to overcome them.

Remember that it is important to link your answers to other topic areas not covered in this chapter.

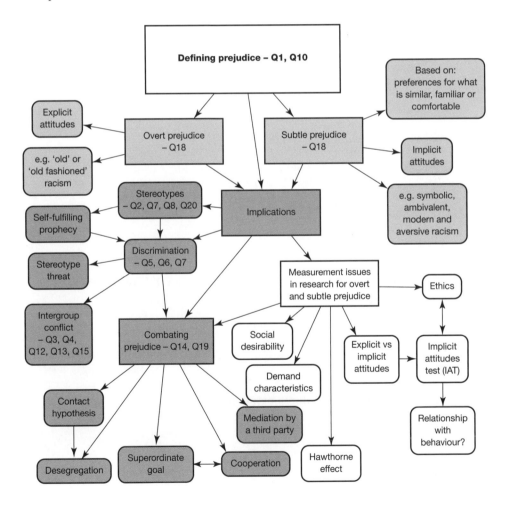

Chapter 8
Gender and sexuality

This chapter covers questions on biological, cultural and evolutionary perspectives of gender and sexuality, gender similarities, differences and roles, sex roles and identities, masculinity, femininity and androgyny, theories of sexuality, and feminist perspectives and critiques.

Select one of the possible answers for each question.

Foundation level questions

1. What does social learning theory suggest regarding children's acquisition of gender roles?

   A. The processes through which children acquire gender roles are more complex than simple learning.

   B. Parents are powerful role models.

   C. Children tend to imitate the behaviour of role models which they observe as being rewarded.

   D. All of the above.

   Your answer:

2. Criticisms of the social learning theory approach to gender role acquisition include which of the following?

   A. Children are viewed by social learning theory as being passive.

   B. Tends to focus too much on behaviour rather than cognition or genetic/ biological factors.

   C. Social learning theory is reductionist in nature.

   D. All of the above.

   Your answer:

3. Which of the following terms is used to refer to biological and reproductive characteristics?

A. Sex.

B. Gender.

C. Sexuality.

D. Femininity/masculinity.

Your answer:

4. What are gender roles?

A. Social constructs used to denote patterns of behaviour typically recognised as 'masculine' or feminine'.

B. Social constructs used to denote people's sexual preferences.

C. The behavioural traits associated with biological sex.

D. Both A and C.

Your answer:

5. The statement 'Women are more oriented toward cooperation and men are more oriented to competition' is an example of what?

A. Social dominance stereotypes.

B. Sexuality-role stereotypes.

C. Sex-role stereotypes.

D. Situational attributions.

Your answer:

6. Much research into gender has focused on two constructs, referred to as what?

A. Strength vs vulnerability.

B. Independence vs connectedness.

C. Adaptation vs disorientation.

D. Automaticity vs control.

Your answer:

7. Which of the following are contemporary perspectives applied to gender and sexuality?

A. Biological.

B. Marxist.

C. Evolutionary.

D. All of the above.

Your answer:

8. Which of Harding's (1986) classifications of feminist approaches to the study of gender essentially argues that women and men may or may not be different, but if accurate measurements on social psychological phenomena are obtained then a more accurate understanding of similarities and differences between the genders will be possible?

A. Feminist standpoint approaches.

B. Feminist empiricist approaches.

C. Feminist constructionist approaches.

D. None of the above.

Your answer:

9. What is the name of the theory that suggests individuals are encouraged to behave in sex-appropriate ways through the social rewards and punishments which are issued by socialising agents and through the identification with other members of the same sex?

A. Social learning theory.

B. The schematic approach.

C. Social identity theory.

D. The self-construal approach.

Your answer:

10. Complete the following sentence:
Heteropatriarchy is a term used to describe the way in which _____ is framed as what is 'normal and natural'.

   A. Homosexuality.

   B. Heterosexuality.

   C. Masculinity.

   D. Femininity.

Your answer: ☐

Advanced level questions

11. Hyde (2005) conducted a review of 46 meta-analyses of research studies looking at gender similarities and differences. Her results suggested what?

   A. That gender differences far outweigh gender similarities.

   B. That gender similarities far outweigh gender differences.

   C. That gender differences and similarities are roughly equal.

   D. That gender differences slightly outweigh gender similarities.

Your answer: ☐

12. Sandra Bem developed the Bem's Sex Role Inventory (BSRI) in the 1970s to measure gender self-appraisal. Why was this controversial at the time?

   A. It questioned the assumption that masculinity and femininity were a dichotomy.

   B. It defined the concept of masculinity and femininity.

   C. Bem suggested the concept of androgyny whereby individuals score equally high on both masculinity and femininity.

   D. Both A and C.

Your answer: ☐

13. Some social constructionist psychologists argue that gender is what?

A. A schema for self-categorisation.

B. Not a stable internal characteristic but existing only in specific social interactions which are understood to be appropriate to one sex.

C. A self-label within a multifaceted construct of self-perceptions such as personality.

D. The result of different social groups and a form of collective identity.

Your answer: [ ]

14. To what does Foucault's (1976) 'strategies to regulate sexuality' refer?

A. Attribution processes used by people to understand other people's sexualities.

B. Self-monitory processes by which individuals make sense of their own sexuality.

C. The historical changes in culture towards sexuality, from free and open to repressed and to supposed liberation.

D. Self-presentation techniques whereby people communicate their sexualities to others.

Your answer: [ ]

15. In the 1990s there was a move towards the discourse analysis approach to exploring gender relations. This was because many psychologists felt it represented what?

A. The opportunity to analyse power relations.

B. An emphasis on gender as a social construction.

C. An approach which is sensitive enough to capture the contextual complexities of gender.

D. All of the above.

Your answer: [ ]

16. Which branch of feminism is associated with the position that women internalise representations of gender where women are relatively powerless (through early life experiences), which become unconscious representations guiding women's behaviour to orient toward nurturing and caring rather than individualistic self-advancement.

A. Psychoanalytic feminism.

B. Liberal feminism.

C. Essentialist feminism.

D. Radical feminism.

Your answer:

17. What does Foucault's approach to understanding sexuality suggest?

A. Sexuality is not an independent entity but is culturally constituted out of the pleasurable possibilities of people's embodiment and discourse.

B. The more we learn about 'sexuality', the more sexually educated people become and the more controlled under a 'regime of bio-power' people become.

C. The term sexuality is misleading; instead the term 'sexualities' should be used to recognise that every person has a sexuality.

D. All of the above.

Your answer:

18. The socialisation of procreative behaviour, the hystericisation of women's bodies, the psychiatrisation of perverse desire and the socialisation of procreative desire are all arguments associated with which influential author?

A. Freud.

B. Foucault.

C. Mitchell.

D. Gilligan.

Your answer:

19. Many new feminist versions of psychoanalytic theory used to explore gender and sexuality are based on the work of Lacan. Which of the following is not one of the three orders through which Lacan argued behaviour is mediated?

A. The imaginary order of unconscious desires and motivations.

B. Symbolic order of language and meaning.

C. Innate forces of the id.

D. The real order of feelings.

Your answer:

20. What does the male warrior hypothesis, developed by Van Vugt (2009), suggest?

A. Intergroup conflicts throughout history have affected the evolved psychologies of men and women differently.

B. Intergroup aggression has typically involved more men than women historically.

C. Men respond more strongly than women to intergroup aggression.

D. All of the above.

Your answer:

Extended multiple-choice question

Complete the following paragraph using the items listed below and overleaf. Not all of the items will be consistent with the paragraph and not all items can be used. Items can be used only once.

_____ (1958) conducted research into men and women's _____ by asking participants to resolve _____ involving male characters. Kohlberg's theory suggested that the highest level of moral reasoning (stage six) involved the development and application of _____, which were abstract in nature. His results revealed that although his _____ participants exhibited this form of moral reasoning, none of his _____ participants did. He concluded that this indicated that women's moral reasoning abilities were _____ as men's. However, another researcher (_____, 1982) highlighted that Kohlberg *assumed* that higher levels of moral reasoning were associated with the application of _____ and that lower levels of moral reasoning were associated with considerations of the _____ of the dilemma (such as helping others). This highlights several issues in research into gender differences: the _____ _____ of asserting differences and the importance of exploring _____ explanations for phenomena such as the different _____ processes underpinning _____.

Optional items

A. Kohlberg

B. ethical considerations

C. moral dilemmas

D. universal ethical principles

E. male

F. gender roles

G. Gilligan

H. abstract principles

I. specific context

J. alternative

K. female

L. not as developed

M. moral reasoning abilities

N. socialisation

Essay questions for Chapter 8

Once you have completed the MCQs above you are ready to tackle some essay questions. You might like to select three or four topics and make notes on them. One way of doing this is to create a concept map. The first question has been done for you and you can see how the knowledge required links to some of the MCQs in this chapter.

1. In what ways have feminist psychological perspectives challenged traditional social psychological theories of gender? Provide examples of key research studies to illustrate your answer.

2. In 2009 Caster Semenya set a new world record in the women's 800 metre race at the World Championships. Her performance was so astonishing that officials ordered her to take a gender identity test which revealed she had three times the level of testosterone expected for a woman. Critically discuss the social psychological implications of this event.

3. Describe and evaluate the concept of sex-role stereotypes. Discuss what implications they have for the social psychological researcher when studying gender.

4. Describe and evaluate the social psychological and feminist psychological approaches to explaining the gap between men and women's average pay.

5. Discuss the suggestion that social dominance is only exhibited by men. Provide examples of relevant psychological theory and research to support your arguments.

6. Critically discuss the ways in which social psychological explanations of gender differences are affected by psychological researchers' cultural beliefs and personal values. In what ways are contemporary social psychological explanations of gender differences and similarities different from classic studies?

7. Compare and evaluate the sociobiological and feminist approaches to understanding sexuality, providing examples of research findings to illustrate their strengths and weaknesses.

8. Some authors argue that the prevalent mainstream constructions of sexuality present it as synonymous with heterosexual ideology and practices. Discuss this position and the implications this may have for research in psychology.

Chapter 8 essay question 1: concept map

In what ways have feminist psychological perspectives challenged traditional social psychological theories of gender? Provide examples of key research studies to illustrate your answer.

The concept map overleaf provides an example of how the first sample essay may be conceptualised. Examination of traditional social psychological theories of gender leads to a number of subtopics, which must each be critically examined before conclusions can be drawn. Comparing this approach with feminist approaches to understanding gender highlights a number of important debates. There are many different feminist psychology perspectives, which have offered different challenges to the way that gender is conceptualised and contextualised (e.g. Marxist and socialist feminist perspectives and the labour market). For a full answer to the question posed, it is necessary to explore each of these feminist perspectives' contributions (and alternative approaches such as discursive psychology) to our understanding of gender (e.g. ideology, conceptualisation and methodology), contrasted with traditional approaches, and to discuss their associated strengths and limitations.

Remember that it is important to link your answers to other topic areas not covered in this chapter.

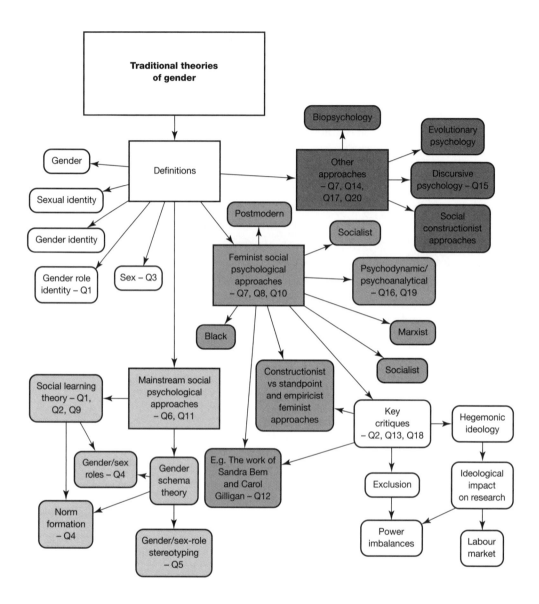

Chapter 9
Close relationships

This chapter includes questions on impression formation (online and offline), attraction and intimacy, what love is, what enables close relationships, how relationships end and how relationship form online.

Select one of the possible answers for each question.

Foundation level questions

1. Which theory suggests that individuals affiliate with other individuals who provide maximum reward for minimal interpersonal cost?

   A. Social exchange theory.

   B. Social comparison theory.

   C. Implicit egotism.

   D. Matching phenomenon.

   Your answer:

2. In an analysis of 166 different cultures, Jankowiak and Fischer (1992) found what percentage showed evidence of a concept of romantic love?

   A. 99%.

   B. 89%.

   C. 79%.

   D. 69%.

   Your answer:

3. Which of the following statements is consistent with the physical attractiveness stereotype?

A. Physically attractive people have lower intelligence than people of average attractiveness.

B. Physically attractive people are more likely to be attracted to other physically attractive people.

C. Physically attractive people are presumed to possess other socially desirable traits as well.

D. All of the above.

Your answer:

4. Which photographs of faces does research consistently suggest are found to be the most attractive?

A. Those faces which are the most distinctive.

B. A composite 'average' of numerous faces.

C. Faces which are similar to that of the person rating them.

D. Faces which are dissimilar to that of the person rating them.

Your answer:

5. Which of the following statements is consistant with an evolutionary approach to understanding attraction?

A. Human preference for attractive partners can be explained in terms of reproductive strategy.

B. Human preference for attractive partners can be explained in terms of socialisation.

C. Human preference for attractive partners can be explained in terms of unequal power structures in society.

D. Both A and C.

Your answer:

6. Which of the following statements is supported by social psychological research?

   A. Attractive people are perceived as likeable.

   B. People whose personalities are described as warm, helpful and considerate have been found to be rated as looking more attractive.

   C. Likeable people are perceived as attractive.

   D. All of the above.

Your answer:

7. When people share similar attitudes, they are more likely to what?

   A. Distrust each other.

   B. Become annoyed with one another because they are too similar.

   C. View each other as more likeable.

   D. Sharing similar attitudes has not been found to have any bearing on interpersonal relationships.

Your answer:

8. The false consensus bias suggests what?

   A. We assume other people share our attitudes, so when we discover that someone has dissimilar attitudes we dislike them.

   B. We assume other people do not share our attitudes, so when we discover that someone has similar attitudes to ourselves we like them.

   C. We assume other people will see us in the same way that we see ourselves, so when we discover information to the contrary we dislike them.

   D. Both A and C.

Your answer:

9. Flattery is an example of what type of strategy?

   A. Deception.

   B. Association.

   C. Ingratiation.

   D. None of the above.

Your answer:

10. Which of the following theories suggests that emotional experience is based on physiological arousal and the cognitive labelling of this experience?

   A. Social exchange theory.

   B. Theory of passionate love.

   C. Two-factor theory.

   D. Balance theory.

Your answer: ☐

Advanced level questions

11. Which of the following is an example of the 'contrast effect'?

   A. When an individual who has been looking at someone deemed 'superattractive' and rates an average looking person (or their own partners) as less attractive than those who have not.

   B. When an individual who has been looking at someone deemed 'superattractive' and rates themselves as less attractive than someone who has not.

   C. When an individual watches pornographic films simulating passionate sex which then leads the individual to feel dissatisfied with their partner.

   D. All of the above.

Your answer: ☐

12. The concept of 'complementarity' (i.e. that opposites attract and that two people in a relationship complete what is missing from the other) has received what?

   A. Little support from social psychological research.

   B. Moderate support from social psychological research.

   C. Great support from social psychological research.

   D. Has not been researched in social psychology.

Your answer: ☐

13. The reward theory of attraction has two principles. The first suggests that we like those whose behaviour is rewarding to us. What does the second principle state?

   A. We like those individuals who appear always to have a positive mood.

   B. We like those individuals whom we associate with good feelings or rewarding events.

   C. We like those individuals who appear to self-censor their behaviour.

   D. None of the above.

Your answer: ☐

14. Eisenberger, Lieberman and Williams (2003) explored the effects of ostracism (acts of exclusion or ignoring another person). What did their results suggest?

   A. Ostracism produces a similar brain response to that triggered by physical pain.

   B. Ostracisim produces a similar brain response to that triggered by confusion.

   C. Ostractism produces a similar brain response to that triggered by fear.

   D. They could find no evidence of the brain response triggered by ostracism.

Your answer: ☐

15. The anticipation of interaction and mere exposure effects are elements of what other effect, known to be a powerful predictor of friendship?

   A. Implicit egotism.

   B. Proximity.

   C. Matching.

   D. Both A and C.

Your answer: ☐

16. Bartholomew and Horowitz (1991) proposed an influential theory of attachment style, based on images of self (positive or negative) and others (positive or negative). Which of the following lists contains all four of these attachment styles?

   A. Secure, dismissing, preoccupied, fearful.

   B. Narcissistic, hedonic, neurotic, histrionic.

   C. Satisfied, dissatisfied, active, passive.

   D. Insecure, accepting, aware, trusting.

Your answer: ☐

17. People from individualist cultures tend to demonstrate a high need for what?

A. Social comparison.

B. Intimacy.

C. Affiliation.

D. Individual 'space' in relationships.

Your answer:

18. Which of the following is an important resource that helps people to cope with the loss of romantic love?

A. Maintaining close contact with the former partner.

B. Being able to dissociate from the memories of the relationship.

C. A supportive social network.

D. Starting a relationship with a new partner shortly following the end of the previous one.

Your answer:

19. Duck (1992) suggested that the dissolution of a relationship is characterised by five phases, through which people move backwards and forwards (rather than progressing in a linear fashion). Which of the following lists contains all five phases?

A. Breakdown, intrapyschic, dyadic, social and grave distressing.

B. Breakdown, polyadic, dyadic, social and termination.

C. Breakdown, polyadic, dyadic, external and grave distressing.

D. Breakdown, intrapyschic, dyadic, social and termination.

Your answer:

20. Gottman (1994, 1998) found that in healthy marriages, positive interactions (such as smiling and complimenting) outnumbered negative interactions (such as sarcasm and insults) by what ratio?

A. 2:1.

B. 3:1.

C. 5:1.

D. 6:1.

Your answer:

Extended multiple-choice question

Using the options listed below complete the following diagram and choose all those statements which can be correctly applied to the model it represents.

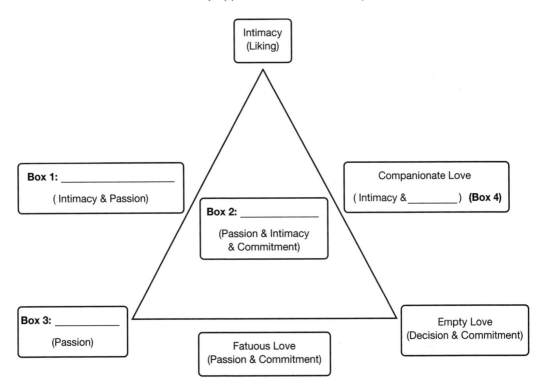

Optional items

A. Romantic love

B. Passionate love

C. Consummate love

D. Intimacy

E. Commitment

F. Passion

G. Infatuation

H. Companionate love refers to the affection felt for those with whom an individual's life is deeply intertwined.

(continued overleaf)

I. Companionate love refers to the intense longing for union with another.

J. This diagram represents Sternberg's (1988) triangular theory of love.

K. This diagram represents the social exchange theory.

L. This diagram represents Hatfield's (1988) theory of passionate love.

Essay questions for Chapter 9

Once you have completed the MCQs above you are ready to tackle some essay questions. You might like to select three or four topics and make notes on them. One way of doing this is to create a concept map. The first question has been done for you and you can see how the knowledge required links to some of the MCQs in this chapter.

1. Describe and evaluate the roles that attachment styles, equity and self-disclosure play in enabling close relationships.

2. Describe and critically discuss the reasons proposed by social psychological research for why people fall in love.

3. Some research suggests that relationships formed online are colder and less fulfilling than relationships formed in face-to-face situations. Critically discuss this suggestion, providing examples of theory and research to support your arguments.

4. Discuss the ways in which relationships may develop differently in online (virtual) environments compared to offline (face-to-face) situations. Provide examples of psychological research and theory to illustrate your answer.

5. Critically examine the ways in which divorce might impact on children's well-being and what the implications might be for their interpersonal adjustment as adults. Provide examples of contemporary psychological research to illustrate your answer.

6. Compare and evaluate the family-systems and interdependence approaches to understanding the process and implications of divorce. Providing examples of research to support your arguments, discuss which approach you believe is most effective.

7. Critically evaluate the role of culture in close relationships. Provide examples of psychological research to illustrate your answer.

8. Compare and evaluate the processes involved in online and offline dating. In what ways are the two situations similar and in what ways might they differ?

Chapter 9 essay question 1: concept map

Describe and evaluate the roles that attachment styles, equity and self-disclosure play in enabling close relationships.

The concept map below provides an example of how the first sample essay may be conceptualised. Examination of the key concepts (defining close relationships, attachment styles, equity and disclosure) reveals a number of subtopics, which must be evaluated before conclusions can be drawn. These topics are interwoven (e.g. equity and self-disclosure) and providing examples which illustrate this (e.g., Computer Mediated Communication research) will allow for a comprehensive picture of the factors enabling close relationships to be presented.

Remember that it is important to link your answers to other topic areas not covered in this chapter.

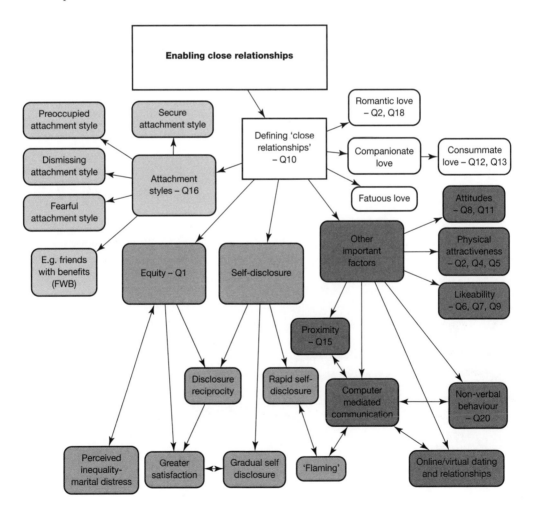

Chapter 10
Methodologies of social psychology

This chapter includes questions on mainstream/experimental social psychological and critical social psychological approaches to research, commonly used methodology, research design and analysis techniques, and their strengths and weaknesses.

Select one of the possible answers for each question.

Foundation level questions

1. Mainstream social psychological researchers are more likely than critical social psychological researchers to use what?

   A. Inferential statistics.

   B. Semi-structured interviewing.

   C. Thematic analysis.

   D. None of the above.

   Your answer:

2. Critical social psychological approaches are more likely to put emphasis on what?

   A. The role of language.

   B. Mundane realism.

   C. Researcher reflexivity.

   D. Both A and C.

   Your answer:

3. The statement 'an integrated set of principles that explain and predict observed events' provides a description of what?

    A. A directional hypothesis.

    B. A non-directional hypothesis.

    C. A theory.

    D. An operationalised definition.

Your answer: ☐

4. For an experiment to have internal validity, which of the following conditions for making causal inferences must it fulfil?

    A. Covariation.

    B. Time-order relationship.

    C. Elimination of plausible alternative causes.

    D. All of the above.

Your answer: ☐

5. Which of the following may arbitrarily affect participants' responses in survey research?

    A. Order of questions.

    B. Response options.

    C. Wording of questions.

    D. All of the above.

Your answer: ☐

6. Which of the following is an example of a participant variable?

    A. Sex.

    B. Religion.

    C. Race.

    D. All of the above.

Your answer: ☐

7. What is the key difficulty encountered when carrying out *true* experimental research in social psychology?

A. Social psychological research often involves 'participant variables', which are ascribed and cannot be manipulated by the research.

B. Often research in social psychology explores situations in which it would be unethical to manipulate variables, for example assigning people with cancer to 'placebo' support conditions. For this reason, natural groups are often used.

C. Social psychology is often particularly interested in exploring relationships and events as they occur naturally, therefore the artificial control of a laboratory experiment may miss the crucial elements of this.

D. All of the above.

Your answer:

8. The way in which a question or issue is posed is known as what?

A. Framing.

B. Positioning.

C. Referencing.

D. Bordering.

Your answer:

9. In social psychological research when should deception be used?

A. Deception can be used in any study as long as participants are debriefed following participation.

B. If the researcher feels that it would produce extremely interesting results.

C. Only if essential and justified by a significant purpose.

D. Deception should never be used.

Your answer:

10. The degree to which an experiment is superficially similar to everyday situations is referred to as what?

   A. Experimental realism.

   B. Mundane realism.

   C. Reliability.

   D. None of the above.

Your answer: ☐

Advanced level questions

11. A researcher conducted a survey exploring university students' perceptions of stress and work-related task-orientation. In both cases, higher scores on the questionnaire indicated a greater degree of the characteristic (i.e. higher levels of stress, greater degree of task-orientation). The researcher reported the following statistical result: $r = -0.83$, $p < 0.5$. Assuming the data was suitable for this statistical procedure, what conclusions can we make about the relationship between the two variables?

   A. There is a strong, statistically significant positive correlation between the variables: as participants' scores on the one scale increase, their scores on the other scale also increase.

   B. There is a strong, statistically significant negative correlation between the variables: as participants' scores on the one scale increase, their scores on the other scale decrease.

   C. There is a weak, statistically significant negative correlation between the variables: as participants' score on the one scale increase, their scores on the other scale decrease.

   D. There is no statistically significant correlation between the two variables.

Your answer: ☐

12. When reporting the results of research psychologists follow different referencing systems. Which of the following is the referencing system used by the British Psychological Society in their research journals?

A. British Psychological Society (BPS).

B. American Psychological Association (APA).

C. Harvard system.

D. Alpha-numeric.

Your answer:

13. Which of the following is an example of quasi-experiments in social psychology?

A. Natural experiments.

B. Participant observation.

C. Field experiments.

D. Both A and C.

Your answer:

14. The extent to which the findings observed in a research study actually reflect processes which occur in natural settings is called what?

A. Internal validity.

B. Ecological validity.

C. Mundane realism.

D. Experimental realism.

Your answer:

15. Cronbach's alpha is a statistical technique commonly used in survey research to assess what?

A. Inter-rater reliability.

B. Internal consistency.

C. External validity.

D. Test-retest reliability.

Your answer:

16. Poor reliability, poor researcher control over the interview, the potential for the interview to not reflect the concerns of the research, high validity and flexibility, are all characteristics associated with which style of interviewing?

A. Structured.

B. Semi-structured.

C. Unstructured.

D. All of the above.

Your answer: ☐

17. The method of sampling most commonly used in qualitative psychological research is what?

A. True random sampling.

B. Stratified random sampling.

C. Purposive.

D. All of these are commonly used in qualitative research.

Your answer: ☐

18. Qualitative psychological research often places greater emphasis than quantitative psychology on what?

A. Researcher reflexivity.

B. The likelihood of events occurring by chance.

C. The role of language.

D. Both A and C.

Your answer: ☐

19. The British Psychological Society's code of ethics and conduct (2009) applies to whom?

A. All psychology students.

B. All members and student affiliates of the BPS.

C. All psychology lecturers, researchers and practitioners.

D. All professionals working with vulnerable adults.

Your answer: ☐

20. Which of the following is not one of the four general ethical principles of the British Psychological Society (2009)?

A. Respect.

B. Competence.

C. Beneficence.

D. Integrity.

Your answer: ☐

Extended multiple-choice question

Complete the following paragraph using the items listed below and opposite. Not all of the items will be consistent with the paragraph and not all items can be used. Items can be used only once.

Constructing a _____ measure for social psychological research involves a number of stages. This includes deciding whether the construct of interest will be measured using a single item (which may be _____) or multiple items (which may be _____). The researcher must also decide whether the questionnaire will be constructed using _____ questions (e.g. those explicitly asking the respondent about their practice of the phenomenon of interest), or _____ measures (for example, asking participants to rate different statements which are believed to be indicators of the construct of interest). This decision will be based, in part, on whether or not the phenomenon the researcher wishes to observe represents a _____, such as an _____. Also, the researcher may believe that direct questions on the specific topic of interest may result in _____ responding, which would affect the _____ of the findings from the results. When constructing a questionnaire, the researcher must also be aware of question _____, such as association effects, which could result in _____ being introduced into the study's results.

Optional items

A. socially representative

B. more reliable

C. direct

D. indirect

E. self-report

F. latent construct

G. order effects

H. socially desirable

I. validity

J. attitude

K. most efficient

L. systematic bias

Essay questions for Chapter 10

Once you have completed the MCQs above you are ready to tackle some essay questions. You might like to select three or four topics and make notes on them. One way of doing this is to create a concept map. The first question has been done for you and you can see how the knowledge required links to some of the MCQs in this chapter.

1. A psychologist's research requires the development and validation of a self-report measure exploring alcohol consumption. Critically examine the issues the psychologist may encounter and the methods they can adopt to overcome them.

2. Compare the self-report survey and direct observation methods when investigating university students' alcohol consumption. Providing evidence to support your argument, discuss which approach you feel would be most effective and why?

3. Describe and discuss the ways that the research methodologies adopted by social psychologists are affected by their philosophical positions.

4. Describe socially desirable responding, demand characteristics and the Hawthorne effect. Critically examine the consequences of these effects for social psychological research and how they can be overcome.

5. What ethical issues must a psychologist consider when designing a research study? Critically evaluate the methods adopted by psychological researchers to overcome them.

6. Compare and evaluate the objectives of quantitative and qualitative psychological research. To what extent do you believe these two approaches to research are mutually exclusive?

7. Critically examine the ways in which the approach taken by an experimental social psychologist and a critical social psychologist in studying teachers' experience of stress may differ. Which approach do you feel would be most effective in this scenario?

8. What factors affect a laboratory experiment's reliability and validity? Critically evaluate the different strategies available to a researcher to mitigate them.

Chapter 10 essay question 1: concept map

A psychologist's research requires the development and validation of a self-report measure exploring alcohol consumption. Critically examine the issues the psychologist may encounter and the methods they can adopt to overcome them.

The concept map below provides an example of how the first sample essay may be conceptualised. There are a number of key issues which must be explored when discussing the development and validation of self-report measures, including: reliability, validity, and question construction. A further angle which will need to be considered in this situation is the ethical implications of developing a questionnaire exploring alcohol consumption (e.g. anonymity), and how these could be managed.

Remember that it is important to link your answers to other topic areas not covered in this chapter.

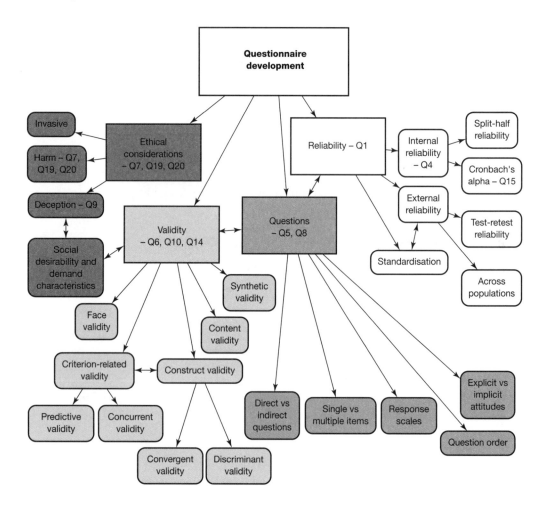

Chapter 11
The discursive self

This chapter includes questions on discursive psychology, the shift towards studying language in its own right, the different approaches to discursive research including discourse analysis and Foucauldian discourse analysis, and their strengths and weaknesses.

Select one of the possible answers for each question.

Foundation level questions

1. Which of the following is *not* a form of discourse analysis?

    A. Conversation analysis.

    B. Critical discourse analysis.

    C. Foucauldian discourse analysis.

    D. Constructive discourse analysis.

    Your answer: ☐

2. What is the key feature of discourse analysis?

    A. It treats discourse (talk and written utterances) as a topic in its own right.

    B. It focuses on process and change as symbolised in speech.

    C. It focuses exclusively on the narrative within a text.

    D. It focuses exclusively on the sequential properties and actions of talk.

    Your answer: ☐

3. From whose work did discursive psychology primarily develop?

    A. Michael Billig and Ian Parker.

    B. Edith Stein and Eugen Fink.

    C. Jonathan Potter and Derek Edwards.

    D. All of the above.

    Your answer: ☐

4. Critical discourse analysis is particularly interested in what?

    A. Talk which demonstrates people's methods of understanding the social world.

    B. Talk which instantiates forms of social or political inequality.

    C. Talk which demonstrates people's conceptions of truth and knowledge.

    D. Talk which grounds people's emotional connections with each other.

Your answer: ☐

5. Which of the following approaches to psychology views talk as primarily argumentative and is particularly interested in persuasive language?

    A. Critical psychology.

    B. Feminist psychology.

    C. Discursive psychology.

    D. Rhetorical psychology.

Your answer: ☐

6. Which of the following is an identity concept commonly studied by discursive researchers?

    A. Place identity.

    B. National identity.

    C. Gendered identity.

    D. All of the above.

Your answer: ☐

7. Discursive psychology operates within which perspective?

    A. Realism.

    B. Relativism.

    C. Positivism.

    D. Empiricism.

Your answer: ☐

8. To which perspective do Foucauldian discourse analysis proponents subscribe?

    A. Critical realism.

    B. Critical relativism.

    C. Social constructionism.

    D. Both A and C.

Your answer:

9. What is a key criticism of discursive psychology?

    A. It is concerned only with public discourse and therefore does not attempt to study internalised manifestations of discourse such as intentionality or self-awareness.

    B. It assumes that everyone in a conversation has a stake in that conversation which they are able to manage.

    C. It cannot say why some individuals or groups pursue certain types of discursive objects or why some people work harder to manage their stake in a conversation than others.

    D. All of the above.

Your answer:

10. In discursive psychological research, what role is the researcher perceived to play?

    A. Author.

    B. Experimenter.

    C. Discoverer.

    D. Witness.

Your answer:

Advanced level questions

11. In discourse analysis, what is 'context'?

   A. The specific passage of talk within which any description is located.

   B. The passage of talk within which any description is located and the broader understanding of what particular words mean.

   C. Exploring the messages within a text and locating them within a historical and social backdrop.

   D. All of the above – there is little consensus on what context is in discourse analysis.

   Your answer:

12. In discursive research, what are conversational identities?

   A. The self-descriptions that people offer within specific instances of text.

   B. Practical actions within talk which allow social interaction to function effectively.

   C. Fluid constructs which alter within different instances of interaction.

   D. All of the above.

   Your answer:

13. In discourse analysis, what form of information should ideally be analysed?

   A. Naturally occurring talk.

   B. Talk arising from semi-structured interviews.

   C. Talk arising from structured interviews.

   D. Any of the above.

   Your answer:

14. When analysing discourse, it is suggested that the researcher should do what?

    A. Commence analysis immediately when reading the transcript through for the first time.

    B. Read the transcript through at least once without attempting analysis.

    C. Choose a random point within the text to start analysis to avoid imposing preconceived conceptions on the data.

    D. Scan through the transcript and only read through information pertaining to specific keywords. All other text should be ignored.

Your answer:

15. What forms of data can Foucauldian discourse analysis be carried out with?

    A. Speech.

    B. Non-verbal behaviour.

    C. Semaphore.

    D. All of the above.

Your answer:

16. In discursive research, what term denotes the immediate surroundings of an interaction such as time and place?

    A. Micro-context.

    B. Macro-context.

    C. Exo-context.

    D. Meso-context.

Your answer:

17. In discourse analysis a 'turn' is what?

    A. A phrase used by an individual which reflects a norm.

    B. An instance within a conversation which serves to change the topic being discussed.

    C. The basic unit of conversation in which one speaker talks.

    D. The basic unit of conversation in which an evaluation occurs.

Your answer:

18. In discourse analysis, 'self-qualifying segments' are what?

A. The non-verbal behaviour aspects of talk (such as hesitancy, clearing your throat) that are used to underscore comments the speaker has just made.

B. Episodes of talk in which the speaker reflexively comments on what they have just said.

C. Episodes of talk in which people use language to display their social status or prestige.

D. Episodes of talk in which the speaker corrects what they have just said.

Your answer: ☐

19. Conversational turns that have narrative elements and follow on from (and are oriented toward) stories produced in preceding turns are called what?

A. Linkages.

B. Memos.

C. Second stories.

D. Aggregated stories.

Your answer: ☐

20. In discourse analysis, what are 'warrants'?

A. The statement of a socially prevailing view of an ideal.

B. An argumentative basis for a claim.

C. An evaluative statement.

D. A justification of socially undesirable behaviour.

Your answer: ☐

Extended multiple-choice question

Complete the following paragraphs using the items listed opposite. Not all of the items will be consistent with the paragraph and not all items can be used. Items can be used only once.

Although there is no single approach to discourse analysis, most approaches follow a similar pattern. For example, analysis tends to focus on the context, _____ and construction of accounts of _____ and subjects. To begin the analysis the first step should be to read through the transcript in _____ and become aware of what the text is _____. Following this, analysis should aim to explore how the talk within the text _____ this purpose.

After reading through the transcript for the first time, the text should be reread and all information relevant to the _____ should be identified. These instances of text are highlighted ready for analysis, or _____. Therefore a '_____' discourse analysis is never actually produced. When reporting discursive research it should be recognised that unlike _____ psychological reports, to facilitate meaningful interpretation of the research findings it is often necessary to merge the analysis and _____ sections.

Optional items

A. variability

B. detail

C. discussion

D. of interest

E. specific research question

F. complete

G. doing

H. accomplishes

I. coding

J. objects

K. quantitative

L. stages

M. its entirety

Essay questions for Chapter 11

Once you have completed the MCQs above you are ready to tackle some essay questions. You might like to select three or four topics and make notes on them. One way of doing this is to create a concept map. The first question has been done for you and you can see how the knowledge required links to some of the MCQs in this chapter.

1. Critically examine discursive researchers' approaches to understanding identity. Provide examples of psychological research to illustrate your answer.

2. Describe and evaluate a discursive psychological approach to exploring prejudice. What might be the strengths and weaknesses of this approach?

3. Compare and evaluate the experimental social psychological and discursive psychological approaches to investigating online (virtual) communication.

4. Critically examine the methodologies adopted by discursive researchers. What are its strengths and weaknesses?

5. Critically compare the discourse analysis and Foucauldian discourse analysis approaches to investigating social phenomena. What are these two approaches' strengths and weaknesses?

6. In what ways are group norms and roles reinforced by discursive practices? Discuss, providing examples of psychological research to support your answer.

7. Critically examine the Foucauldian discourse analysis approach to language. What are its strengths and weaknesses?

8. Compare the perspectives of Foucauldian discourse analysis and discursive psychology on the role of language in social phenomena. What are the implications of this comparison?

Chapter 11 essay question 1: concept map

Critically examine discursive researchers' approaches to understanding identity. Provide examples of psychological research to illustrate your answer.

The concept map below provides an example of how the first sample essay may be conceptualised. Examination of the key discursive approaches in social psychology reveals a number of subtopics, including the different epistemological and ontological considerations underlying them and the subsequent differences in analysis methods which tend to be adopted. Considering these topics reveals differences in the way that language is conceptualised (e.g. a means of constructing the world, or managing stakes in the social world), the role researchers play (e.g. an author) and ultimately how psychological and social processes are understood (e.g. difficulties exploring internal mental states or intentions). Examining the strengths and limitations of the different approaches, and the ways in which researchers manage these, will provide a full answer to the question posed.

Remember that it is important to link your answers to other topic areas not covered in this chapter.

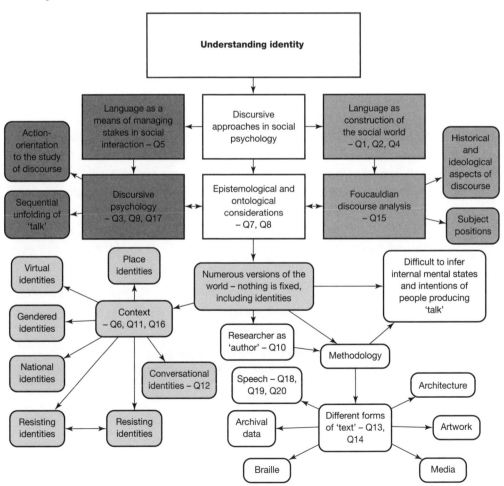

Writing an essay: a format for success

When writing an essay on a topic in social psychology, it is important to remember that social psychology is not a unified discipline; there are many different approaches, such as mainstream (also referred to as traditional or experimental) social psychology, critical social psychology, discursive psychology and feminist social psychologies to name but a few. Each of these different branches approach the study of social processes and phenomena in different ways, are associated with different methodologies and have impacted on traditional social psychological theories. A good essay will incorporate information on these different approaches, where appropriate (i.e. always ensure your answer addresses the question set), and discuss the impact they have had on the understanding of the social processes in question. Remember, to write a good essay you need to do more than merely describe the issues at hand: you need to impartially present both sides of the discussion and then clearly and concisely state where your position lies and why, providing evidence from relevant examples of research and theory to support your arguments.

It is important to recognise that when addressing topics in social psychology, you will need to define the constructs in question, describe the relevant theories and evaluate them using evidence from research to explore their strengths and weaknesses. Although it is important to demonstrate knowledge of the key classic studies related to the understanding (or development) of a theory, a strong essay will include relevant contemporary research as well; this demonstrates that you are up to date with topical debates in the field. Also, topics within social psychology (such as 'attitudes') often represent a mix of theory, basic and applied research. This presents you with a good opportunity to demonstrate not only that you are aware of theories of the mechanisms underpinning social processes, but can also demonstrate your ability to apply these theories to 'real life' scenarios.

Remember, a good essay only includes information which is relevant to the question actually asked. So, once you have drafted an essay reread it and make sure that your arguments are focused and that each point you have made addresses the topic in question. If you cannot see how it is relevant, neither will an examiner or marker.

Scoring methods in MCQs

Introduction

All assessments need to be reviewed and marked. At your university you will come across a number of formal (often called summative) and informal (aka formative) assessments. These can take the form of practical reports, essays, short-answer questions and (of course) examinations. There are, of course, a number of forms of examinations – short answers, written essays and multiple-choice questions (or MCQs).

MCQs are considered objective assessments, that is answers are unambiguously correct or incorrect and therefore provide for high marker reliability – so that's one positive mark for MCQs. On the other hand, there is often a concern (for the examination setter) that guessing by the candidate can have an inflationary influence on the marks. By chance, if you have four choices then you should score 25% just by guessing. This is obviously not a situation to be encouraged, and because of this your psychology course team may have introduced various attempts to make sure that this does not happen. It is worth exploring some of these methods and the implications these will have for the approach you take to your assessment and, ultimately, how they can impact on your examination performance.

Scoring of MCQ examinations can take several forms. At its most simple, a raw score is calculated based on the total number of correct responses (usually 1 mark per correct answer). Under this approach, any omissions or incorrect responses earn you no marks but neither do they attract a penalty. If you get the question right, you get a mark; if you do not then you get no mark.

As mentioned, alternative and more complex approaches to marking have been developed because of concerns that results can be inflated if correct responses are the result of successful guessing. The most common approaches to discouraging random guessing include the reward of partial knowledge and negative marking. This can impact on your behaviour and your learning. Of course, whatever the examination and whatever the marking scheme, you need to know your stuff!

Rewarding partial knowledge

Scoring procedures developed to reward partial knowledge are based on the assumption that though you and your student colleagues may be unable to identify a single correct response you can confidently identify some options as being incorrect and that partial knowledge should therefore be rewarded. Versions of this approach generally allow you to choose:

- more than one possibly correct response and to be awarded a partial mark provided one of your responses is the correct answer;
- a 'not sure' option for which you are awarded a proportion of a mark (usually either 0.2 or 0.25).

Negative marking

Negative marking is when your performance is based on the total number of correct responses which is then reduced in some way to correct for any potential guessing. The simplest application of negative marking is where equal numbers of marks are added or subtracted for right and wrong answers and omitted answers, or the selection of a 'No answer' option that has no impact on marks. So, you get +1 mark when you get the question right, –1 mark when you get it wrong and 0 if you do not attempt it. However, there are other approaches which are slightly more punitive. In these approaches, if you get the question correct you get +1, if you get the question wrong then this is awarded a –1 (or even –2) and if there is no attempt then this is awarded a –1 as well as, it is suggested, you do not know the answer.

How does this impact on you?

The impact of these scoring mechanisms can be significant. By way of example, use the following table to demonstrate your performance in each of the chapters in this text. For each of the chapters work out the number of correct responses (and code this as NC), the number of incorrect answers (coded as NI) and the number of questions that you did not provide a response to (NR). You can then use the formulae in the table to work out how you would have performed under each of the different marking schemes. For example, for the punitive negative marking scheme you score 18 correct (NC=18), 2 incorrect (NI=2) and omitted 5 questions (NR=5). On the basis of the formula in the table, NC-(NI*2)-NR, you would have scored 9 (i.e. 18-(2*2)-5). So even though you managed to get 18 out of 25 this would have been reduced to only 9 because of the punitive marking.

Chapter	Number correct	Number incorrect	No response	Marking scheme: raw score	Marking scheme: partial knowledge	Marking scheme: negative marking	Marking scheme: punitive negative marking
	NC	NI	NR	= NC	= NC – (NI * 0.2)	= NC – NI	= NC – (NI * 2) – NR
1							
2							
3							
4							
5							
6							
7							
8							
9							
10							
11							
TOTAL							

Explore the scores above – which chapter did you excel at and for which chapter do you need to do some work? Use the above table to see your areas of strength and areas of weakness – and consequently where you need to spend more time revising and reviewing the material.

MCQ answers

Chapter 1: Introduction to social psychology – MCQ answers

Level	Question number	Correct response	Self-monitoring
Foundation	1	C	
Foundation	2	B	
Foundation	3	A	
Foundation	4	D	
Foundation	5	C	
Foundation	6	C	
Foundation	7	A	
Foundation	8	D	
Foundation	9	B	
Foundation	10	B	
Advanced	11	C	
Advanced	12	C	
Advanced	13	B	
Advanced	14	A	
Advanced	15	A	
Advanced	16	D	
Advanced	17	C	
Advanced	18	A	
Advanced	19	B	
Advanced	20	C	
		Total number of points:	Foundation: Advanced:

EMCQ for Chapter 1

The paragraph should read as follows. A maximum of 11 points can be awarded.

A distinction needs to be made between modernist and postmodernist approaches to social psychology. <u>Modernism</u> is based on the assumption that <u>science</u> is the only way in which rational knowledge can be gained. However, <u>postmodernism</u> argues that knowledge is <u>constructed</u> rather than <u>discovered</u> and is <u>multiple</u> rather than <u>singular</u>. Postmodernist proponents argue that knowledge is not ideologically <u>neutral</u> and is in fact a means by which <u>power</u> is exercised. It can be seen that <u>mainstream</u> social psychology is aligned with modernist principles, whereas <u>critical</u> social psychology is aligned with postmodernist principles.

Chapter 2: Understanding social identities – MCQ answers

Level	Question number	Correct response	Self-monitoring
Foundation	1	C	
Foundation	2	B	
Foundation	3	B	
Foundation	4	C	
Foundation	5	D	
Foundation	6	A	
Foundation	7	A	
Foundation	8	A	
Foundation	9	C	
Foundation	10	D	
Advanced	11	A	
Advanced	12	B	
Advanced	13	C	
Advanced	14	D	
Advanced	15	A	
Advanced	16	A	
Advanced	17	C	
Advanced	18	C	
Advanced	19	D	
Advanced	20	B	
		Total number of points:	Foundation: Advanced:

EMCQ for Chapter 2

The paragraph should read as follows. A maximum of 10 points can be awarded.

A person's <u>social identity</u> (which is based on social groups to which they belong) should be differentiated from their <u>personal identity</u> (relating to an individual's unique and idiosyncratic features which appear unrelated to group membership). Two key theories which explore the mechanisms underpinning social identity are the social identity theory (by <u>Tajfel and Turner, 1986</u>) and self-categorisation theory (<u>Turner, Hogg, Oakes, Reicher and Wetherell, 1987</u>). Social identity theory proposes that we form our social identity from the group memberships which are <u>important</u> to us. This theory suggests we derive <u>self-esteem</u> from this social identity, through the derogation of <u>outgroups</u>. Self-categorisation theory suggests that our group memberships influence our social identity, <u>self-concept</u> and <u>behaviour,</u> through processes such as <u>conformity</u>.

Chapter 3: Making attributions – MCQ answers

Level	Question number	Correct response	Self-monitoring
Foundation	1	C	
Foundation	2	B	
Foundation	3	A	
Foundation	4	A	
Foundation	5	C	
Foundation	6	D	
Foundation	7	B	
Foundation	8	A	
Foundation	9	C	
Foundation	10	D	
Advanced	11	A	
Advanced	12	B	
Advanced	13	B	
Advanced	14	C	
Advanced	15	D	
Advanced	16	B	
Advanced	17	D	
Advanced	18	B	
Advanced	19	B	
Advanced	20	C	
		Total number of points:	Foundation: Advanced:

EMCQ for Chapter 3

The paragraph should read as follows. A maximum of 10 points can be awarded.

Both the <u>fundamental attribution error</u> theory and the <u>actor-observer effect</u> refer to <u>biases</u> in the way people make attributions. However, they make different suggestions about the way people think; the fundamental attribution error states people have a tendency to attribute the actions of other people to <u>internal dispositions or traits</u>. However, the actor-observer effect refers to the fact that an <u>actor</u> is more likely to make situational attributions regarding a task they are completing, whereas an <u>observer</u> is more likely to make dispositional attributions about the individual. For example, a student might make the <u>situational attribution</u> that they are studying for an exam because the <u>exam will be difficult</u> whereas an observer may make the <u>dispositional attribution</u> that the <u>student is a hard worker</u>.

Chapter 4: Attitudes – MCQ answers

Level	Question number	Correct response	Self-monitoring
Foundation	1	D	
Foundation	2	D	
Foundation	3	C	
Foundation	4	B	
Foundation	5	B	
Foundation	6	C	
Foundation	7	A	
Foundation	8	C	
Foundation	9	D	
Foundation	10	D	
Advanced	11	C	
Advanced	12	A	
Advanced	13	C	
Advanced	14	B	
Advanced	15	D	
Advanced	16	A	
Advanced	17	A	
Advanced	18	C	
Advanced	19	B	
Advanced	20	A	
		Total number of points:	Foundation: Advanced:

EMCQ for Chapter 4

A maximum of 7 points can be awarded.

Correct answers for boxes:

Box 1: B.   Attitude toward the behaviour.

Box 2: D.   Intention.

Box 3: F.   Behaviour.

Correct statements:

     C.   This is an example of an expectancy-value model.

     E.   The model was later modified to include 'perceived behavioural control'.

     G.   The adapted model became known as the 'theory of planned behaviour'.

     H.   Attitude toward the behaviour is defined as the sum of expectancy × value products.

Chapter 5: Social influence – MCQ answers

Level	Question number	Correct response	Self-monitoring
Foundation	1	C	
Foundation	2	A	
Foundation	3	D	
Foundation	4	A	
Foundation	5	B	
Foundation	6	B	
Foundation	7	D	
Foundation	8	D	
Foundation	9	C	
Foundation	10	D	
Advanced	11	C	
Advanced	12	A	
Advanced	13	D	
Advanced	14	C	
Advanced	15	D	
Advanced	16	D	
Advanced	17	C	
Advanced	18	B	
Advanced	19	D	
Advanced	20	D	
		Total number of points:	Foundation: Advanced:

EMCQ for Chapter 5

The paragraph should read as follows. A maximum of 11 points can be awarded.

Cults represent important <u>groups</u> to study in social psychology because they represent examples of extreme persuasion. Cults typically share three characteristics which facilitate this persuasion. Firstly, they involve members making commitments to the cult <u>publicly</u> and repeatedly, a mechanism by which behaviour influences attitudes through the <u>internalisation</u> of the commitments. Secondly, they involve 'social implosion': isolating members from their external ties so they only have contact with other like-minded individuals. This isolation leads to a loss of <u>counter-arguments</u>, increased group <u>cohesion</u> and consensus and ultimately this sense of collective identity leads to increased <u>conformity</u>. Cult leaders often apply the principles of <u>effective</u> persuasion: appearing <u>credible</u> and charismatic, using varied, <u>vivid</u> and emotional forms of communication and deliberately targeting individuals who may be more vulnerable to their persuasion efforts (for example, targeting people under the age of 25 whose values and attitudes are still developing). It is important to recognise that, despite all these factors, cults do not automatically recruit people and their efforts of persuasion can be resisted through techniques such as <u>attitude inoculation</u>.

Chapter 6: Group processes – MCQ answers

Level	Question number	Correct response	Self-monitoring
Foundation	1	D	
Foundation	2	B	
Foundation	3	D	
Foundation	4	C	
Foundation	5	D	
Foundation	6	B	
Foundation	7	D	
Foundation	8	A	
Foundation	9	C	
Foundation	10	A	
Advanced	11	C	
Advanced	12	A	
Advanced	13	C	
Advanced	14	A	
Advanced	15	D	
Advanced	16	D	
Advanced	17	A	
Advanced	18	B	
Advanced	19	D	
Advanced	20	A	
		Total number of points:	Foundation: Advanced:

EMCQ for Chapter 6

The paragraph should read as follows. A maximum of 8 points can be awarded.

In 1898 Triplett conducted one of the first ever <u>laboratory</u> experiments in social psychology. He asked children, either on their own or among a group of other children, to <u>wind string on a reel</u> as fast as they could. Triplett found that children who performed the task among other children were <u>quicker</u> (an example of an <u>audience effect</u>). He therefore suggested that the mere presence of other people is enough to enhance task performance, an effect he called <u>social facilitation</u>. However, other research found the opposite could also be true. Therefore in 1965 <u>Zajonc</u> modified the theory to suggest that the presence of other people results in <u>evaluation apprehension</u>, which will lead to the enhancement of the <u>dominant response tendency</u>. Therefore, in a simple task, the social facilitation effect will result in greater confidence and increased performance, but in a complex task this will result in greater anxiety and a decrease in performance.

Chapter 7: Prejudice – MCQ answers

Level	Question number	Correct response	Self-monitoring
Foundation	1	B	
Foundation	2	C	
Foundation	3	A	
Foundation	4	A	
Foundation	5	B	
Foundation	6	C	
Foundation	7	D	
Foundation	8	C	
Foundation	9	B	
Foundation	10	B	
Advanced	11	C	
Advanced	12	C	
Advanced	13	B	
Advanced	14	A	
Advanced	15	B	
Advanced	16	D	
Advanced	17	A	
Advanced	18	D	
Advanced	19	D	
Advanced	20	D	
		Total number of points:	Foundation: Advanced:

EMCQ for Chapter 7

The paragraph should read as follows. A maximum of 10 points can be awarded.

There are two main types of prejudice, which are known as subtle (largely <u>unconscious</u>) and overt (<u>conscious</u>). These two different types of prejudice require different methods to measure and detect them. For example, to detect subtle prejudice researchers have needed to develop <u>discrete survey questions</u> and <u>indirect</u> measures, such as the <u>implicit association test (IAT)</u>. There is evidence to suggest that although explicit attitudes may change dramatically through <u>education,</u> implicit attitudes are more resistant and may only change through <u>practice</u> and <u>new habits</u>. There is also evidence to suggest that different areas of the brain are implicated in automatic prejudice and conscious prejudice: the <u>amygdala</u> (a primitive region of the brain associated with fear) is associated with unconscious prejudice, whereas the <u>frontal cortex</u> (which is associated with conscious thinking) is associated with more conscious prejudice.

Chapter 8: Gender and sexuality – MCQ Answers

Level	Question number	Correct response	Self-monitoring
Foundation	1	D	
Foundation	2	D	
Foundation	3	A	
Foundation	4	A	
Foundation	5	C	
Foundation	6	B	
Foundation	7	D	
Foundation	8	B	
Foundation	9	A	
Foundation	10	B	
Advanced	11	B	
Advanced	12	D	
Advanced	13	B	
Advanced	14	C	
Advanced	15	D	
Advanced	16	A	
Advanced	17	D	
Advanced	18	B	
Advanced	19	C	
Advanced	20	D	
		Total number of points:	Foundation: Advanced:

EMCQ *for Chapter 8*

The paragraph should read as follows. A maximum of 14 points can be awarded.

Kohlberg (1958) conducted research into men and women's moral reasoning abilities by asking participants to resolve moral dilemmas involving male characters. Kohlberg's theory suggested that the highest level of moral reasoning (stage six) involved the development and application of universal ethical principles, which were abstract in nature. His results revealed that although his male participants exhibited this form of moral reasoning, none of his female participants did. He concluded that this indicated that women's moral reasoning abilities were not as developed as men's. However, another researcher (Gilligan, 1982) highlighted that Kohlberg *assumed* that higher levels of moral reasoning were associated with the application of abstract principles and that lower levels of moral reasoning were associated with considerations of the specific context of the dilemma (such as helping others). This highlights several issues in research into gender differences: the ethical considerations of asserting differences and the importance of exploring alternative explanations for phenomena such as the different socialisation processes underpinning gender roles.

Chapter 9: Close relationships – MCQ answers

Level	Question number	Correct response	Self-monitoring
Foundation	1	A	
Foundation	2	B	
Foundation	3	C	
Foundation	4	B	
Foundation	5	A	
Foundation	6	D	
Foundation	7	C	
Foundation	8	A	
Foundation	9	C	
Foundation	10	B	
Advanced	11	D	
Advanced	12	A	
Advanced	13	B	
Advanced	14	A	
Advanced	15	B	
Advanced	16	A	
Advanced	17	C	
Advanced	18	C	
Advanced	19	A	
Advanced	20	C	
		Total number of points:	Foundation: Advanced:

EMCQ for Chapter 9

A maximum of 6 points can be awarded.

Correct answers for boxes:

Box 1:   A.   Romantic love

Box 2:   C.   Consummate love

Box 3:   G.   Infatuation

Box 4:   E.   Commitment

Correct statements:

H.   Companionate love refers to the affection felt for those with whom an individual's life is deeply intertwined.

J.   This diagram represents Sternberg's (1988) conception of kinds of loving.

Chapter 10: Methodologies of social psychology – MCQ answers

Level	Question number	Correct response	Self-monitoring
Foundation	1	A	
Foundation	2	D	
Foundation	3	C	
Foundation	4	D	
Foundation	5	D	
Foundation	6	D	
Foundation	7	D	
Foundation	8	A	
Foundation	9	C	
Foundation	10	B	
Advanced	11	B	
Advanced	12	B	
Advanced	13	D	
Advanced	14	B	
Advanced	15	A	
Advanced	16	C	
Advanced	17	C	
Advanced	18	D	
Advanced	19	B	
Advanced	20	C	
		Total number of points:	Foundation: Advanced:

EMCQ for Chapter 10

The paragraph should read as follows. A maximum of 11 points can be awarded.

Constructing a <u>self-report</u> measure for social psychological research involves a number of stages. This includes deciding whether the construct of interest will be measured using a single item (which may be <u>most efficient</u>) or multiple items (which may be <u>more reliable</u>). The researcher must also decide whether the questionnaire will be constructed using <u>direct</u> questions (e.g. those explicitly asking the respondent about their practice of the phenomenon of interest), or <u>indirect</u> measures (for example, asking participants to rate different statements which are believed to be indicators of the construct of interest). This decision will be based, in part, on whether or not the phenomenon the researcher wishes to observe represents a <u>latent construct</u>, such as an <u>attitude</u>. Also, the researcher may believe that direct questions on the specific topic of interest may result in <u>socially desirable</u> responding, which would affect the <u>validity</u> of the findings from the results. When constructing a questionnaire, the researcher must also be aware of question <u>order effects</u>, such as association effects, which could result in <u>systematic bias</u> being introduced into the study's results.

Chapter 11: The discursive self – MCQ answers

Level	Question number	Correct response	Self-monitoring
Foundation	1	D	
Foundation	2	A	
Foundation	3	C	
Foundation	4	B	
Foundation	5	D	
Foundation	6	D	
Foundation	7	B	
Foundation	8	D	
Foundation	9	D	
Foundation	10	A	
Advanced	11	D	
Advanced	12	D	
Advanced	13	A	
Advanced	14	B	
Advanced	15	D	
Advanced	16	A	
Advanced	17	C	
Advanced	18	B	
Advanced	19	C	
Advanced	20	B	
		Total number of points:	Foundation: Advanced:

EMCQ for Chapter 11

The paragraphs should read as follows. A maximum of 10 points can be awarded.

Although there is no single approach to discourse analysis, most approaches follow a similar pattern. For example, analysis tends to focus on the context, <u>variability</u> and construction of accounts of <u>objects</u> and subjects. To begin the analysis the first step should be to read through the transcript in <u>its entirety</u> and become aware of what the text is <u>doing</u>. Following this, analysis should aim to explore how the talk within the text <u>accomplishes</u> this purpose.

After reading through the transcript for the first time, the text should be reread and all information relevant to the <u>specific research question</u> should be identified. These instances of text are highlighted ready for analysis, or <u>coding</u>. Therefore a '<u>complete</u>' discourse analysis is never actually produced. When reporting discursive research it should be recognised that unlike <u>quantitative</u> psychological reports, to facilitate meaningful interpretation of the research findings it is often necessary to merge the analysis and <u>discussion</u> sections.